Editor

Erica N. Russikoff, M.A.

Editor in Chief

Ina Massler Levin, M.A.

Creative Director

Karen J. Goldfluss, M.S. Ed.

Cover Artist

Brenda DiAntonis

Imaging

James Edward Grace
Craig Gunnell

Publisher

Mary D. Smith, M.S. Ed.

TCR 2558

STRATE...
to use with your
English Language Learners

4-6

Contains TESOL Goals and Standards

- Includes ELL strategies for teachers and students
- Tailored to help ELLs as well as native English speakers
- Provides sample activities and lessons across the content areas

Teacher Created Resources

Author

Tracie I. Heskett, M. Ed.

Teacher Created Resources

6421 Industry Way
Westminster, CA 92683
www.teachercreated.com

ISBN: 978-1-4206-2558-5

© 2012 Teacher Created Resources
Made in U.S.A.

Teacher Created Resources

Table of Contents

Table of Contents *(cont.)*

Introduction

Teachers across the country are experiencing increasing numbers of English language learners (ELLs) in their regular education classrooms. As ELL student populations grow, teachers need strategies to reach these students. Many lessons in existing curricula are designed for native speakers of English and are not tailored to support second language acquisition. The lessons and strategies in this book accommodate the needs of ELLs.

Strategies to Use With Your English Language Learners offers teachers ways to teach specific concepts and skills to ELLs and at-risk students in regular education classrooms. This book includes charts with ELL strategies, teaching methods, suggested activities, and sample lessons.

The following are a few of the most frequently asked questions regarding ELL instruction. The answers provided are general; for more specific answers, review the strategies in this book.

How do specific strategies help ELLs?

Literacy strategies support ELLs as they build English proficiency. Supporting students' first language skills helps students develop literacy in English. Effective teaching strategies engage students and increase their motivation to learn.

What should I do if some students already know the lesson content?

Assess students and use that information to design lesson plans and objectives. Determine what students already know and what they need to know. Include ways to differentiate teaching and activities in the lesson if some students already know part of the lesson content. Encourage students to use what they already know to extend ideas and ask questions about the lesson topic.

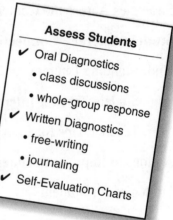

Assess Students
- ✔ Oral Diagnostics
  - • class discussions
  - • whole-group response
- ✔ Written Diagnostics
  - • free-writing
  - • journaling
- ✔ Self-Evaluation Charts

How do I reteach if students don't grasp the concept the first time?

Ask questions and check student work throughout the lesson. Provide concrete examples and ask students to give their own examples. Be aware of ways that students' native languages may influence their learning of English. This will allow you to target areas in which students need direct instruction. Try to identify other aspects of the lesson that might cause difficulty for ELLs, and give explanations as needed.

How can I use interactive whiteboard technology to help my ELLs?

Interactive whiteboard technology can be an invaluable resource when working with ELLs. ELL instruction is often visually oriented; pictures, graphics, and other visual information help to increase student comprehension. Use interactive whiteboard technology to enhance the following:

- ✦ add variety to visual aids and graphic organizers.
- ✦ provide sentence frames for different language levels.
- ✦ display charts and tables.
- ✦ help students make connections between written and oral text.
- ✦ engage students in cloze activities.

How to Use This Book

The first section, *Developing a Multicultural Classroom*, provides tips and resources to develop a multicultural environment in the classroom. It contains information about working with parents, including a sample parent letter. This section also offers specific steps for integrating English language learners, including how to build cultural awareness, increase verbal interaction, and motivate students.

The second section, *English Language Learner Instruction*, contains information on collaborating with ESL staff, recognizing learning styles, and differentiating lessons. It also addresses specific strategies teachers can use with their ELLs. A few of the strategies you'll find in this section are Dialogue Journals, Environmental Print, and Reciprocal Teaching. Each strategy page includes an explanation, examples, tips for teaching, and at least one sample activity.

The third section, *Student Literacy Connections*, consists of student and teacher tips to increase literacy, as well as student strategies. Teach your students these strategies so they can use them independently to increase their reading comprehension. A few of the strategies you'll find in this section are Clarifying, Making Inferences, and Using Context Clues. Each strategy page includes an explanation, tips for teaching, and ways to use the strategy across the content areas (reading, writing, social studies, and science).

The final section, *Across the Curriculum*, contains vocabulary tips and activities, acknowledging that students need academic and content-area vocabulary to succeed in school. This section also includes reading, writing, social studies, and science activities; sample lessons; and information on assessment. The resources, activities, and sample lessons provided will help you to incorporate ELL teaching strategies into lessons across the content areas.

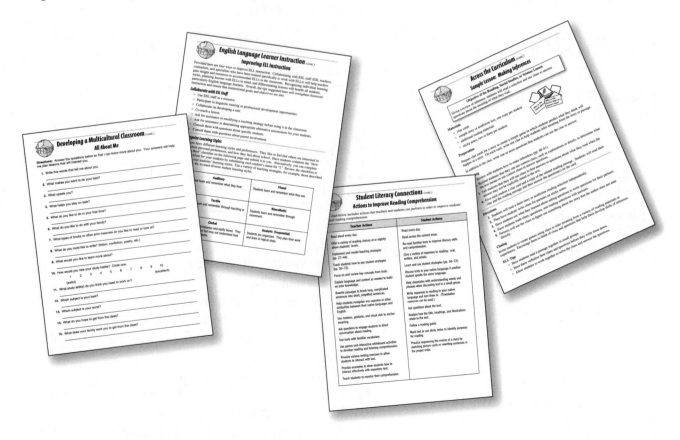

Correlation to TESOL Standards

The following chart lists the Teachers of English to Speakers of Other Languages (TESOL) goals, standards, and descriptors for Pre-K–12 students. (Reprinted with permission of TESOL, from *ESL Standards for Pre-K–12 Students, Online Edition*, 2010; permission conveyed through Copyright Clearance Center, Inc.)

Goals and Standards	Descriptors
Goal 1. To use English to communicate in social settings **Standard 1.** Students will use English to participate in social interactions	1. share and request information 2. express needs, feelings, and ideas 3. use nonverbal communication in social interactions 4. get personal needs met 5. engage in conversations 6. conduct transactions
Goal 1. *(cont.)* **Standard 3.** Students will use learning strategies to extend their communicative competence	2. listen to and imitate how others use English 3. explore alternative ways of saying things 4. focus attention selectively 5. seek support and feedback from others 6. compare nonverbal and verbal cues 7. self-monitor and self-evaluate language development 8. use the primary language to ask for clarification 9. learn and use language "chunks" 10. select different media to help understand language 11. practice new language 12. use context to construct meaning
Goal 2. To use English to achieve academically in all content areas **Standard 1.** Students will use English to interact in the classroom	1. follow oral and written directions, implicit and explicit 2. request and provide clarification 3. participate in full-class, group, and pair discussions 4. ask and answer questions 6. negotiate and manage interaction to accomplish tasks 7. explain actions 8. elaborate and extend other people's ideas and words
Goal 2. *(cont.)* **Standard 2.** Students will use English to obtain, process, construct, and provide subject matter information in spoken and written form	1. compare and contrast information 2. persuade, argue, negotiate, evaluate, and justify 3. listen to, speak, read, and write about subject matter information 4. gather information orally and in writing 5. retell information 6. select, connect, and explain information 7. analyze, synthesize, and infer from information 9. represent information visually and interpret information presented visually 10. hypothesize and make predictions 12. understand and produce technical vocabulary and text features according to content area 13. demonstrate knowledge through application in a variety of contexts

Correlation to TESOL Standards *(cont.)*

Goals and Standards	Descriptors
Goal 2. *(cont.)* **Standard 3.** Students will use appropriate learning strategies to construct and apply academic knowledge	**2.** apply basic reading comprehension skills such as skimming, scanning, previewing, and reviewing text **4.** take notes to record important information and aid one's own learning **6.** determine and establish the conditions that help one become an effective learner **7.** plan how and when to use cognitive strategies and apply them appropriately to a learning task **8.** actively connect new information to information previously learned **9.** evaluate one's own success in a completed learning task **12.** know when to use native language resources (human and material) to promote understanding
Goal 3. To use English in socially and culturally appropriate ways **Standard 1.** Students will use the appropriate language variety, register, and genre according to audience, purpose, and setting	**1.** use the appropriate degree of formality with different audiences and settings **2.** recognize and use standard English and vernacular dialects appropriately **3.** use a variety of writing styles appropriate for different audiences, purposes, and settings **7.** determine when it is appropriate to use a language other than English **8.** determine appropriate topics for interaction
Goal 3. *(cont.)* **Standard 2.** Students will use nonverbal communication appropriate to audience, purpose, and setting	**1.** interpret and respond appropriately to nonverbal cues and body language **2.** demonstrate knowledge of acceptable nonverbal classroom behaviors **3.** use acceptable tone, volume, stress, and intonation in various social settings **4.** recognize and adjust behavior in response to nonverbal cues
Goal 3. *(cont.)* **Standard 3.** Students will use appropriate learning strategies to extend their sociolinguistic and sociocultural competence	**1.** observe and model how others speak and behave in a particular situation or setting **2.** experiment with variations of language in social and academic settings **3.** seek information about appropriate language use and behavior **4.** self-monitor and self-evaluate language use according to setting and audience **5.** analyze the social context to determine appropriate language use **6.** rehearse variations of language use in different social and academic settings

ESL Terms

The following are some of the most common terms used in ESL instruction. These terms are repeated throughout the book. For definitions of specific strategies (e.g., environmental print, scaffolding, paraphrasing), look on pp. 27–44 and 50–72.

Academic language: language used in the school environment, including words, phrases, grammar, and language structure, as well as academic terms and technical language

BICS: Basic Interpersonal Communication Skills (See pg. 11 for an extensive definition.)

Bilingual: speaking two languages fluently

CALP: Cognitive Academic Language Proficiency (See pg. 11 for an extensive definition.)

Chunks/Chunking: information divided into units in order to be more comprehensible

Cognates: words in different languages related to the same root (e.g., *education* [English] and *educación* [Spanish])

Content area: refers to academic subjects in school (e.g., math, science, English/language arts, reading, and social studies)

Decoding: skills used (such as transfer) to decipher given information into understandable information

Differentiated instruction: modified instruction so that students of different abilities, knowledge, and skills can equally experience materials (e.g., providing multiple assignments within a teaching unit that are tailored for students with differing language levels) (See pg. 25 for more information.)

EFL: English as a Foreign Language

ELL: English Language Learner

ESL: English as a Second Language

Explicit instruction: otherwise known as "direct instruction"; learners are provided with specific information or directions about what is to be learned.

Fluency: ability to read, write, and speak a language easily, naturally, and accurately

Language acquisition: the natural process of learning a language; second language acquisition usually includes formal study

Language proficiency: ability to communicate and understand oral (listening and speaking) and written (reading and writing) academic and nonacademic language (See pg. 9 for the English Language Proficiency levels.)

Multicultural: relating to multiple cultural groups (See pp. 13–20 for information on multicultural classrooms.)

Native language: first language learned and spoken

Native speakers of English (or native English speakers): individuals whose first language is English

Realia: real objects used for tactile demonstrations and for improving students' understanding (e.g., bringing in real flowers when teaching about plants)

Transfer (as in language transfer): applying knowledge and skills from a first language to a second language

Wait time: amount of time that elapses between a question or instruction and the next verbal response

Levels of English Language Proficiency

This checklist will help you determine an ELL's proficiency as he or she develops English skills and progresses from one level to the next.

Student Name: _____   **Date:** _____

❑ Level 1–Entering

- ✦ Responds to content-area pictures and graphics
- ✦ Understands and speaks words, phrases, or "chunks" of language (with errors)
- ✦ Understands one-step commands and directions
- ✦ Understands yes-no and WH-questions (pg. 50)
- ✦ Requires visual or graphic support

❑ Level 2–Beginning

- ✦ Responds to general content-area language
- ✦ Understands and speaks phrases and short sentences (with errors)
- ✦ Understands multiple-step commands and directions
- ✦ Understands multiple-step questions and statements
- ✦ Requires some visual or graphic support

❑ Level 3–Developing

- ✦ Responds to general and some specific content-area language
- ✦ Understands, speaks, and writes expanded sentences (with errors)
- ✦ Understands and writes paragraphs (with errors)
- ✦ Requires occasional visual or graphic support

❑ Level 4–Expanding

- ✦ Responds to specific and some technical content-area language
- ✦ Understands, speaks, and writes sentences of varying lengths (with minimal errors)
- ✦ Understands and writes multiple-paragraph assignments (with minimal errors)
- ✦ Requires occasional visual or graphic support

❑ Level 5–Bridging

- ✦ Responds to technical content-area language
- ✦ Understands, speaks, and writes sentences of varying lengths
- ✦ Understands and writes multiple-paragraph stories, essays, or reports
- ✦ Performs close to grade-level expectations in reading, writing, and content-area skills

The Four Language Domains

TESOL's language proficiency standards are divided into four language domains: listening, speaking, reading, and writing. They are listed in the order in which students become proficient. Below each language domain are activities targeted to support language development.

Listening

- ✦ Provide recorded texts for students to practice listening.
- ✦ Have students listen and respond to American TV shows and movies.
- ✦ Provide focused read-aloud experiences.
- ✦ Teach songs, chants, and jingles for student participation.
- ✦ Read poetry to help students learn how language sounds.
- ✦ Place students in pairs, giving each partner a different list of words or sentences. Have students take turns reading their lists and documenting the words or sentences. Check for accuracy.
- ✦ Give students dictation.

Speaking

- ✦ Increase student interaction time.
- ✦ Ask open-ended questions.
- ✦ Remind students to speak clearly.
- ✦ Provide practice with speaking in different tenses.
- ✦ Ask students about their cultures as they relate to topics of discussion.
- ✦ Encourage students to elaborate on peer responses.
- ✦ Have students participate in dialogues.

Reading

- ✦ Set a purpose for reading.
- ✦ Use a variety of books for a unit of study.
- ✦ Set aside time each day for sustained silent reading (SSR), allowing students to choose their own texts.
- ✦ Teach students how to skim while reading.
- ✦ Have students practice reading song lyrics.
- ✦ Have students practice reading quietly before they read aloud.
- ✦ Have students read subtitles while watching an American TV show or movie.

Writing

- ✦ Model how to use different tenses in writing.
- ✦ Model correct grammar.
- ✦ Have students write personal responses to texts.
- ✦ Have students practice writing simple sentences, adding details to them at a later time.
- ✦ Have students participate in whole-class or small-group writing.
- ✦ Encourage students to practice writing at home in journals.
- ✦ Allow students to make choices in what they write (notes to friends or family members, stories, autobiographical pieces).

Types of Language Acquisition: BICS and CALP

ELLs acquire English on two different levels: social and academic. Teachers may hear struggling students speaking naturally with classmates and wonder why they continue to have trouble with schoolwork. It's important to understand that students acquire social language skills (BICS) before academic language proficiency (CALP). What this means is that, although students may be conversationally (BICS) fluent, they have not necessarily mastered academic language skills (CALP). Continue to familiarize your ELLs with classroom concepts in order to increase their academic language proficiency.

BICS–Basic Interpersonal Communication Skills

- ◆ used with friends and family
- ◆ used in face-to-face conversations
- ◆ more informal
- ◆ has short sentences
- ◆ provides contextual clues
- ◆ not cognitively demanding

CALP–Cognitive Academic Language Proficiency

- ◆ used in the classroom and with texts
- ◆ used to express abstract concepts
- ◆ more formal
- ◆ contains complicated grammar, technical vocabulary, and multiple-meaning words
- ◆ lacks context
- ◆ more cognitively demanding
- ◆ may have idioms and figurative language
- ◆ contains words and phrases that describe content-area knowledge and procedures
- ◆ expresses higher-order thinking processes (e.g., inferring, evaluating)

The Importance of CALP in Classroom Instruction

Academic language skills help students to do the following:

- ✦ develop new knowledge.
- ✦ improve literacy.
- ✦ increase test performance.
- ✦ understand abstract concepts.
- ✦ solve problems.
- ✦ make decisions.

- ✦ use written language.
- ✦ use higher-order thinking skills.
- ✦ read textbooks.
- ✦ ask and respond to questions.
- ✦ participate in lessons.
- ✦ work in collaborative groups.

Teachers can help ELLs learn academic language by doing the following:

- ✦ providing explicit instruction.
- ✦ teaching students the difference between BICS and CALP.
- ✦ recognizing when students need a BICS word to replace a CALP word and modifying the text accordingly.
- ✦ creating a chart of CALP words and related BICS phrases relevant to the classroom and textbooks.
- ✦ introducing and explaining skills daily.
- ✦ targeting instruction to specific skills.
- ✦ clarifying directions.
- ✦ introducing academic terms in context.
- ✦ explaining the meaning of academic words.
- ✦ using academic language in classroom speech.
- ✦ displaying terms in the classroom for student reference.
- ✦ teaching complex sentence structures.
- ✦ pointing out grammatical features to help students understand text.
- ✦ providing sentence frames that support students' use of academic language.
- ✦ incorporating pair work, allowing students with strong English skills to work with students who need support.
- ✦ providing study groups for students to review textbook topics.

CALP words	BICS words
analyze collaborate	look at work together

Students can learn academic language by doing the following:

- ✦ reading words in context to learn the meaning.
- ✦ looking for visual cues.
- ✦ categorizing words into everyday use and academic use.
- ✦ paying attention to keywords or phrases that are repeated.
- ✦ noticing facial expressions when someone else reads.

Developing a Multicultural Classroom
Home-School Connections

A multicultural classroom is one in which students from a variety of cultural backgrounds feel welcome and safe. Multicultural teachers have an awareness of their students' diverse backgrounds and pass on that cultural awareness to all of their students. As teachers practice empathy and give students opportunities to work in their native languages as well as English, they help students learn a new language. Teachers further build a multicultural environment by encouraging a strong connection between the students' lives at school and at home.

Parents want the best for their children and are concerned about their well-being, particularly at school. Translation resources make it possible for teachers to communicate with family members in their native languages, read notes students bring from home, and allow students to communicate in their native languages as needed to understand new concepts. The following resources can help teachers connect with family members of ELLs:

- ✦ ESL specialists or ESL teachers
- ✦ interpreters
- ✦ bilingual students
- ✦ community members
- ✦ computer programs
- ✦ online resources (pg. 110)

Using these resources, teachers, students, and parents can each help create and maintain a strong, positive connection between home and school.

Specifically, teachers can also do the following:

- ✦ send home a (translated, if necessary) parent note for family discussion to preteach a concept.
- ✦ teach theme units around ELLs' countries, national food, or other cultural topics; compare and contrast two or more cultures.
- ✦ group students by native language for student conferences and provide interpreters as available.
- ✦ include pictures and other visual aids in parent conferences.
- ✦ encourage parents to hold students accountable for completing homework.

Specifically, students can do the following:

- ✦ ask family members questions about how their cultures relate to topics of study.
- ✦ keep reading journals in their native languages.
- ✦ share family experiences related to topics of current learning.
- ✦ share common expressions from their cultures and relate them to idioms they've learned in English.

Specifically, parents can do the following:

- ✦ share areas of expertise with students through artistic, oral, or written messages.
- ✦ ask students questions in their native languages about what they are learning.
- ✦ assist students with schoolwork by asking questions and discussing assignments in their native languages.
- ✦ attend student conferences (with translation assistance, if necessary).

Developing a Multicultural Classroom *(cont.)*
Sample Parent Letter

Adapt the following letter to fit your teaching situation. Translation assistance may be available for parents who wish to share their experiences with the class. Create a brief explanation of routines, procedures, and expectations specific to your class. As needed, enlist the aid of an ESL specialist or teacher, interpreter, computer software, or online resource to translate parent letters.

Dear Parent or Guardian:

Welcome to our classroom! We hope you and your child will enjoy exploring new learning together.

The following list suggests ways you can help your child do well in school:

   ✎ Help your child find a time and place to do homework.

   ✎ Ask your child questions, or have him or her read to you.

   ✎ Invite your child to ask you questions.

   ✎ Ask your child to show you how to do something new that he or she has learned to do.

   ✎ Talk with your child about what he or she is learning at school—in any language.

Perhaps you have experience or an area of special knowledge that you can share with our class. You might know how to prepare a special meal or do a particular trade or craft. Perhaps you have another skill or job experience that relates to a current topic of learning. I would like to hear about it. Translation assistance is available if needed. I look forward to getting to know you better.

Included with this letter is a brief explanation of our classroom procedures. I hope this will help make school easier for your child.

           Sincerely,

Developing a Multicultural Classroom *(cont.)*
8 Steps for Integrating English Language Learners

As teachers receive more and more ELLs into their classrooms, it's important that they learn to integrate them with the rest of their student population. The following eight steps will help you with this process. Instructional goals for ELLs include helping them use English to communicate and learn. As teachers increase their awareness of the cultural diversity their students bring to the classroom, they can get to know and support ELLs as they learn a second language in an academic setting. Comprehensible instruction and opportunities for verbal interaction will motivate students to engage in learning and actively participate in classroom activities.

❶ Create a Supportive Environment

✦ Make students feel comfortable and welcome.

✦ Create a predictable, structured classroom environment.

✦ Reduce student anxiety through positive reinforcement, acceptance, and cultural awareness.

✦ Create an environment that accepts more than one way to do things.

✦ Hold high expectations for academic work and student behavior.

✦ Communicate expectations positively to students.

✦ Write expectations on a chart for display.

✦ Respect all language varieties; it might not be "academic language," but it is still valuable for students' communication in other social settings (e.g., home, playground, outside of class).

✦ Orient students to available classroom resources (e.g., bilingual dictionaries).

❷ Get to Know Your Students

✦ Use formative assessments, such as journals, quick writes, or rough drafts.

✦ Use the "All About Me" questionnaire (pg. 19) to learn about your students' interests and backgrounds.

✦ Create a weekly class newsletter. For each edition, focus on a different student.

❸ Build Cultural Awareness

✦ Support and appreciate your students' cultures.

✦ Know which qualities and characteristics a student's culture values.

✦ Understand culturally acceptable ways of intervention in times of community, family tragedy, or student difficulty.

✦ Acknowledge and support diversity.

✦ Know the strengths and benefits of diversity and share them with your students.

✦ Use books, posters, websites, and videos to build diversity into an existing curriculum.

✦ Learn a few words and phrases in your students' native languages, if possible.

❸ Build Cultural Awareness *(cont.)*

✦ Build on students' background knowledge (culture, traditions, music, historical figures, family, personal interests).

✦ Connect learning to students' families and cultures.

✦ Incorporate ways to learn about different cultures into classroom instruction and discussion.

✦ Use examples and information from various cultures to illustrate concepts.

✦ Learn about cultural differences and incorporate them into classroom activities.

✦ Use materials that feature students' cultural groups.

✦ Use materials in students' native languages or at their levels of English proficiency.

✦ Encourage students to share about their cultures with the class.

✦ Allow students to use their native languages for some tasks.

✦ Draw on the diverse cultural, social, and linguistic resources of students and use them as strengths in the classroom.

✦ Read multicultural literature in class, and have it available for students to read independently.

❹ Help Students Learn a New Language

✦ Imagine what it would be like to be an ELL, learning and functioning in a second language.

✦ Enable students to feel secure and willing to take risks with language.

✦ Have students speak in small groups to give them authentic speaking opportunities with real listeners.

✦ Encourage direct responses from students.

✦ Help students to understand that they are adding a new language, not replacing their native languages and cultures.

✦ Develop students' knowledge base in their first languages to strengthen their ability to learn a new language.

✦ Offer translation assistance.

✦ Keep a picture dictionary handy for reference.

✦ Teach language in context.

✦ Expose Entering and Beginning ELLs to Bridging ELLs. (See pg. 9.)

✦ Know the language patterns for ELLs' languages; compare them to English language patterns, and give students opportunities to practice English patterns.

✦ Provide classroom materials in a wide range of reading levels.

❺ Use Comprehensible Instruction

✦ Give directions in "chunks."

✦ Preteach vocabulary.

✦ Speak slowly and use slower pacing of lessons.

✦ Allow for wait time, or time for students to think, during student responses.

✦ Use repetition, especially in commands and instructions.

✦ Build context around a new word or concept.

✦ Question students to make sure they understand concepts and tasks.

✦ Use motions, gestures, and facial expressions to communicate.

✦ Use visual aids.

✦ Structure lessons to leave enough time for students to practice and demonstrate what they have learned.

✦ Incorporate what students already know into lesson plans.

❻ Increase Verbal Interaction

✦ Ask open-ended questions.

✦ Provide opportunities for class discussions.

✦ Repeat what students say to show that you understand.

✦ Have students explain how they know which answer is the best choice.

✦ Incorporate partner and group work.

  • Have students interview each other.

  • Have students explain concepts and processes to each other.

  • Pair an ELL with a native English speaker.

  • Place students in trios with one ELL, one student who speaks the ELL's native language and English, and one native English speaker.

✦ Encourage students to interact with and summarize text.

✦ Encourage students to communicate ideas and ask questions.

✦ Encourage students to think of more than one answer for a prompt.

7 **Provide Opportunities for Active Student Involvement**

✦ Engage students in lessons using manipulative materials and realia (three-dimensional objects from real life).

✦ Provide hands-on activities for students so they can learn by doing.

✦ Conduct open-ended investigations.

✦ Offer activities at multiple levels so all students can participate.

✦ Give students choices of activities and assignments.

✦ Build on the knowledge, skills, and experiences students bring to class.

✦ Allow students to use methods other than reading and writing to obtain information and express what they have learned.

✦ Encourage students to work independently when appropriate.

✦ Have students participate in cooperative learning activities in small groups.

8 **Motivate ELLs for Success**

✦ Positively reinforce the contributions ELLs make in class.

✦ Provide fun projects and tasks with their own rewards.

✦ Consider classroom contests with prizes, if appropriate.

✦ Plan classroom activities to match student interests and abilities.

✦ Encourage students' desires to impress. Suggest they complete a task with someone they respect as the audience.

✦ Use accountability charts to help students stay on track.

✦ Challenge students and give them reasons to do the following:

  • learn the language.

  • understand stories and other texts.

  • establish social relationships and make friends.

  • communicate wants, needs, and feelings.

  • take part in activities.

  • help organize activities.

  • share their cultures with classmates who are native English speakers.

Directions: Answer the questions below so that I can know more about you. Your answers will help me plan lessons that will interest you.

1. Write five words that tell me about you.

    _____

2. What makes you want to do your best?

    _____

3. What upsets you?

    _____

4. What helps you stay on task?

    _____

5. What do you like to do in your free time?

    _____

6. What do you like to do with your family?

    _____

7. What types of books or other print materials do you like to read or look at?

    _____

8. What do you most like to write? (fiction, nonfiction, poetry, etc.)

    _____

9. What would you like to learn more about?

    _____

10. How would you rate your study habits? Circle one.

          1   2   3   4   5   6   7   8   9   10

       (awful)   (excellent)

11. What study skill(s) do you think you need to work on?

    _____

12. Which subject is your best?

    _____

13. Which subject is your worst?

    _____

14. What do you hope to get from the class?

    _____

15. What does your family want you to get from the class?

    _____

Developing a Multicultural Classroom (cont.)
Am I a Multicultural Teacher?

Think about your role in the classroom. Read the questions below and mark a "✔" in the boxes that match your actions. Reflect on the answers to help you better meet your students' needs.

❏ Do I make students feel comfortable and welcome?

❏ Have I created a predictable, structured classroom environment?

❏ Have I communicated expectations positively to students?

❏ Do I use formative assessments, such as journals, quick writes, or rough drafts?

❏ Have I learned about my students' interests and backgrounds?

❏ Do I support and appreciate my students' cultures?

❏ Do I connect learning to students' families and cultures?

❏ Do I use examples and information from various cultures to illustrate concepts?

❏ Do I read multicultural literature in class and have it available for students to read?

❏ Have I imagined what it's like to be an ELL, learning and functioning in a second language?

❏ Do I have students speak in small groups to give them authentic speaking opportunities?

❏ Do I provide classroom materials in a wide range of reading levels?

❏ Do I preteach vocabulary?

❏ Do I question students to make sure they understand concepts and tasks?

❏ Do I use visual aids?

❏ Do I structure lessons to leave enough time for students to practice and demonstrate what they have learned?

❏ Do I provide opportunities for class discussions?

❏ Do I repeat what students say to show that I understand?

❏ Do I incorporate partner and group work?

❏ Do I engage students in lessons using manipulative materials and realia?

❏ Do I provide hands-on activities for students so they can learn by doing?

❏ Do I offer activities at multiple levels so all students can participate?

❏ Do I positively reinforce the contributions ELLs make in class?

❏ Do I use accountability charts to help students stay on track?

❏ Do I challenge students and give them reasons to learn the language?

English Language Learner Instruction
Helping Struggling ELLs

English language learners may quickly fall behind in their comprehension, even though it appears they are completing their work in class. Becoming aware of the needs of ELLs also means knowing when they have difficulty in class. The examples below are representative of students who no longer understand classroom instruction. If you have students that display one or more of the following behaviors, review the Teacher's Responsibilities list below and help your ELLs overcome these obstacles to comprehension.

When students struggle, they may exhibit one or more of the following behaviors:

- be silent.
- demonstrate nonverbal behaviors.
- be inattentive.
- not feel part of the classroom community.
- not ask for help.
- create discipline issues.

- seek attention.
- have low reading and writing skills.
- not understand instruction easily.
- find it harder to concentrate on the lesson.
- do poorly on tests.
- have potential but lack confidence to apply their learning.

Students' Responsibilities	Teacher's Responsibilities
Reach for excellence.	Know your expectations for ELLs and other students.
Realize that it's OK to not be successful in everything.	Provide scaffolding (pg. 40) and partnership for each student.
Find ways to improve.	Repeat directions or reteach.
Ask for help when needed.	Give additional explanation if needed.
Use time well.	Provide wait time, or time for ELLs to respond when prompted, acknowledging that students are processing new information and participating in higher-level thinking.
Set and monitor learning goals.	
Learn to listen.	
Participate.	Prompt students to use specific reading strategies.
	Observe students during work time and note which students have decoding or comprehension problems.
	Note students' progress in meeting reading and language objectives.
	Intervene quickly when students are off-task, and call on them to participate.
	Ask questions at different levels of difficulty.
	Work in smaller groups with those students who have difficulty.

English Language Learner Instruction *(cont.)*
Improving ELL Instruction

Provided here are four ways to improve ELL instruction. Collaborating with ESL staff (ESL teachers, counselors, and specialists who have been trained specifically to work with ELLs) will help teachers gain insight and resources to accommodate ELLs in the classroom. Recognizing individual learning styles, planning lessons with ELLs in mind, and differentiating lessons will benefit all students, particularly English language learners. Overall, the tips suggested here will strengthen classroom instruction and ensure that instructional goals and objectives are met.

Collaborate with ESL Staff

- ✦ Use ESL staff as a resource.
- ✦ Participate in linguistic training or professional development opportunities.
- ✦ Collaborate on developing a unit.
- ✦ Co-teach a lesson.
- ✦ Ask for assistance in modifying a teaching strategy before using it in the classroom.
- ✦ Ask for assistance in determining appropriate alternative assessments for your students.
- ✦ Consult them with questions about specific students.
- ✦ Consult them with questions about parent involvement.

Recognize Learning Styles

Students have different learning styles and preferences. They like to feel that others are interested in them, their personal preferences, and how they feel about school. Have students complete the "How I Learn Best" checklist on the following page and submit it to you. Alternatively, you can complete the checklists for your students by substituting each student's name for "I." Review the checklists to identify your students' learning styles. Use a variety of teaching strategies, for example, those described on pp. 27–44, to meet diverse student learning styles.

Auditory Students learn and remember what they hear.	**Visual** Students learn and remember what they see.
Tactile Students learn and remember through touching or feeling.	**Kinesthetic** Students learn and remember through movement.
Global Students are spontaneous and easily bored. They see the big picture but may not understand how they arrive at answers.	**Analytic (Sequential)** Students are organized. They plan their work and learn in logical steps.

English Language Learner Instruction *(cont.)*

Improving ELL Instruction *(cont.)*

How I Learn Best

Directions: Each statement below describes how someone learns. Add a "✔" next to the statements that are true for you. Your answers will help me plan lessons that will be easier for you to learn.

- ❏ Reading together as a group helps me remember what was read.
- ❏ I can remember what I learn if I make a model or draw a picture.
- ❏ It helps if new information is given with movements.
- ❏ I can learn by looking at things.
- ❏ I like to do science experiments.
- ❏ I like to talk about things in class with a small group.
- ❏ I can remember details easily.
- ❏ I like to read aloud.
- ❏ I like to role-play or act out things we learn in class.
- ❏ It helps if I have something to look at when the teacher is talking.
- ❏ Graphic organizers (webs, Venn diagrams, etc.) help me organize my thoughts.
- ❏ Instructions that are said out loud are easy for me to understand and remember.
- ❏ It is easier to remember directions and other information if I copy it for myself.
- ❏ I would rather give an oral report than write a report on paper.
- ❏ I like activities in which I can move things around.
- ❏ I can work by myself.
- ❏ Games help me remember new information.
- ❏ I like to help plan and organize group projects or my own work.
- ❏ Written instructions are easy for me to understand and remember.
- ❏ I can remember what teachers say if they use hand motions.
- ❏ I like to work in groups.
- ❏ It is easier for me to remember new information if it is presented in a logical order.
- ❏ I do well on assignments and tests that have listening sections.
- ❏ I like to read new information silently to myself.
- ❏ I can understand a writing assignment better if we practice as a whole group.
- ❏ A checklist helps me see the big picture for a project.
- ❏ Watching videos helps me learn new information.
- ❏ Step-by-step directions make it easy for me to follow along.
- ❏ I like it when the teacher gives us new information.

Plan Lessons with ELLs in Mind

✦ Use standards as a guide to determine what ELLs need to learn.

✦ Pre-assess students' knowledge and skill levels.

✦ Set instructional goals and learning objectives based on what students still need to know.

✦ Display objectives for students so they know what is expected.

✦ Determine what students need to do to accomplish learning tasks. Share this information with students.

✦ Provide a lesson outline for students to follow.

✦ Preview lesson objectives and activities with students.

✦ Provide a list of target words for the lesson or unit.

✦ Use the same icons throughout a lesson to cue students.

✦ When teaching a new strategy, describe what the strategy is, why it should be learned, and when, where, and how the strategy should be used.

✦ Connect learning in one subject area to learning in another subject area.

✦ Give each activity a name that describes it.

✦ Create a visual aid while talking, such as a chart, table, or drawing (pg. 44); use an interactive whiteboard.

✦ Break lessons into "chunks."

✦ Allow time for students to write notes or responses.

✦ Incorporate multilevel teaching.

✦ Provide a summary and review of the lesson in one or two sentences.

✦ Encourage students to get help with assignments at school.

✦ Document student performance to gauge students' needs.

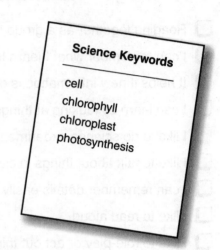

Science Keywords

cell
chlorophyll
chloroplast
photosynthesis

Differentiate Lessons

✦ Differentiate based on skill levels:

- Some students are better speakers.

- Some students are better readers.

- Some students are better writers.

✦ Match lessons and activities to students' learning styles. Use the "How I Learn Best" handout (pg. 23) to help you meet the needs of your students.

✦ Recognize that students may not all be doing the same activity at the same time.

✦ Give students choices of activities when possible.

✦ Allow students to work at their own pace within guidelines.

✦ Consider behavior management issues.

✦ Provide bilingual activities or resources to help students complete tasks successfully.

✦ Encourage students to explore topics in a variety of ways.

✦ Help students master study skills.

✦ Address the abilities, needs, interests, and strengths of learners.

✦ Model a concept orally or in writing for the whole class (pg. 37).

✦ Use peer tutoring (pg. 38), buddy systems, or team projects.

✦ Use the same reading text for the whole class, adapt activities, and provide direct guided instruction for ELLs.

✦ Adapt required reading activities for two or three levels.

✦ Give students an easy reading task when text is difficult.

✦ Give students a more challenging reading task when the text is easy.

✦ Have students read about the same topic at their own reading levels.

✦ Modify oral tasks based on ELLs' oral fluency.

English Language Learner Instruction *(cont.)*
Tips for Using Teaching Strategies

The following tips will help you integrate strategies when planning lessons:

✦ Use ELL strategies with all students.

✦ Teach students strategies they can use to help themselves learn.

✦ Use sticky tabs to mark pages in order to quickly reference specific strategies.

✦ Write an ELL tip or strategy in your lesson plan book for one or more lessons during the day.

✦ Make cards for the "Extending Vocabulary" strategies (pp. 74–78) or "Strategies Across the Content Areas" (pp. 45–46).

✦ Create cards for any of the other charts in this book as a quick reference.

✦ Consider making cards with various activities for students to choose from based on their learning styles and preferences.

How to incorporate strategy cards into daily teaching:

✦ Keep the cards in a small file box.

✦ Hole-punch cards and place them on a ring for handy reference.

✦ Post one or two cards daily at your desk as a quick visual reminder of strategies to use with ELLs.

✦ Take a few minutes to review one or two cards each morning. In a month, you'll be familiar with several strategies and can draw on them as needed.

English Language Learner Instruction *(cont.)*
Teaching Strategies

Brainstorming

Use this strategy to activate students' prior knowledge. Have students think of as many answers to a question or problem as possible, and then write down everyone's ideas.

Examples: webs, lists (e.g., ways to use an object), clustering, K-W-L charts (pg. 35), mind maps, story maps, diagrams, word association, note-taking, categorizing information (i.e., grouping related items), asking questions (pg. 50), discussing ideas with classmates, drawing pictures to generate ideas

Tips for Teaching the Strategy

- ✦ When compiling students' ideas, make sure everyone can see the diagram.
- ✦ Encourage all students to participate. Model respect for all contributors.
- ✦ Consider a small motivational incentive to encourage ELLs to participate in sharing their ideas aloud.

Sample Activity

Introduce a unit on inventions by placing students in groups. Give each group an assortment of odds and ends, such as rubber bands, paper clips, tape, scratch paper, etc. Invite students to create inventions with their building materials. Have groups share and explain their inventions with the class. Discuss the process students used to create the new inventions, and compare it to how real inventions are created.

Choral Reading

Use this strategy to increase fluency and reading comprehension skills. Choral reading provides support for struggling readers, encourages them to take risks, and builds their confidence. Have students read in unison as a class or in small groups. Afterwards, discuss the selection and have students re-read the text together.

Ways to Use Choral Reading: for chants, jingles, songs, poetry, readers' theater (pg. 42), nonfiction text (rewritten as scripts), patterned or predictable text, rhyming or rhythmic text

Tips for Teaching the Strategy

- ✦ Use actions and gestures to reinforce the meaning of the text.
- ✦ Use as a differentiated instruction activity by pairing students of different abilities together.
- ✦ Have students take turns leading.
- ✦ Have students practice choral reading until they can use the strategy with partners or in small groups.

Sample Activity

Divide the class into small groups. Perform a choral reading of a poem, with each group reciting a different stanza. Discuss the poem at its end or after each stanza (depending upon length), and then recite the poem as a class.

English Language Learner Instruction (cont.)
Teaching Strategies (cont.)

Cloze Activities

Use this strategy to allow students to actively participate in reading. Prepare a passage with blanks substituted for specific words. Have students substitute words that make sense. Use this strategy in these ways:

✦ to teach or review specific aspects of language or grammar.

✦ as a pre-reading activity to set a purpose for reading.

✦ to engage students in academic reading.

✦ to help students learn new words and build comprehension and vocabulary.

Examples: fill-in-the-blank passages with word banks, fill-in-the-blank sentences that correspond with an audio file or video, fill-in-the-blank tests

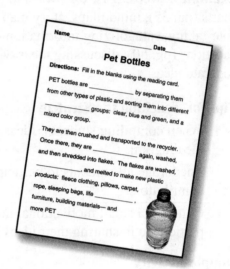

Tips for Teaching the Strategy

✦ Cover part of the word or sentence.

✦ Provide a word bank.

✦ Give the starting letter of the word.

✦ Provide written or oral activities.

✦ Use with a whole group or have students work independently.

Sample Activity

Prepare a cloze activity that corresponds with a TV show or short movie. Watch the show ahead of time and transcribe dialogue (verbatim). Replace keywords with blanks. Test your students' listening comprehension by having them watch the video and fill in the blanks.

Cooperative Groups

Use this strategy to help students develop critical-thinking skills in a structured learning environment. Cooperative groups focus on student-centered learning and increase student interaction time. Have students work together on a shared task in small groups.

Ways to Use Cooperative Groups: during brainstorming (pg. 27), answering questions, problem solving, projects that demonstrate learning

Tips for Teaching the Strategy

✦ Clearly define the task.

✦ Assign or rotate individual student roles within the groups.

✦ Hold students accountable individually for their own work; have each team turn in a group project, as well.

Sample Activity

Have students work together as a group to create an imaginary country. Include any components related to an actual social studies unit of study.

English Language Learner Instruction *(cont.)*
Teaching Strategies *(cont.)*

Dialogue Journals

Use this strategy to help students participate in interactive writing on an individual basis. A dialogue journal is an informal conversation between two or more people. It reinforces learning while also forming bonds. For students who feel more comfortable writing than speaking, this strategy gives them the opportunity to join in an ongoing conversation. Use dialogue journals to do the following:

- ◆ respond to students' questions and comments.
- ◆ ask students questions.
- ◆ introduce new concepts.
- ◆ clarify information.

Ways to Use Dialogue Journals: when analyzing specific literary components (plot, characters) or devices (imagery, symbolism), sharing predictions, comparing and contrasting (pg. 53)

Tips for Teaching the Strategy

- ◆ Journal partners do not have to be teachers. Students can correspond with classroom aides, each other, or with students who are in another grade level or are more proficient in English.
- ◆ Model correct grammar, spelling, and punctuation when corresponding with students.

Sample Activity

Set up dialogue journals to discuss a current literature book selection or academic topic.

DLTA (Directed Listening-Thinking Activity)

Use this strategy to have students listen to and make predictions throughout a text. This strategy builds on what students already know and shows them how to apply this knowledge to new situations. Teachers should read aloud at the highest level students can understand, bearing in mind that students can comprehend at higher levels than they can read. After reading aloud a passage, invite students to submit evidence to support their predictions and conclusions.

Ways to Use DLTA: during the reading of fiction stories, nonfiction text, text that students cannot yet read independently

Tip for Teaching the Strategy

Have students make predictions in the form of questions and then notice how those questions were answered in the text.

Sample Activity

Have students write their predictions early in the activity. Pause throughout the reading to ask questions, and have students generate additional predictions. Have students take notes and revise their original predictions as necessary. After reading, have students participate in a think-pair-share activity (pg. 43) in which they write one or two sentences concluding what they heard and how it relates to their predictions before sharing with partners.

DRTA (Directed Reading-Thinking Activity)

Use this strategy to model how to make and confirm predictions. Here are the steps to DRTA:

1. Choose a text. Preselect stopping points where students can pause while reading.
2. Preview keywords or pictures. Ask questions to guide students' thinking.
3. Have students make predictions about what they will read (pp. 62–63).
4. Stop at set points so students can check predictions, revise them (as needed), and make new predictions.
5. Ask questions to help students match their predictions to their actual reading.
6. Discuss what has been read before reading the next section.

Examples: Use objects or pictures to preview a text and make predictions; ask questions about keywords and vocabulary (pg. 50); focus on characters and what they might do; determine the author's purpose in writing; observe headings to predict what the reader might learn.

Tips for Teaching the Strategy

 ✦ Use as a whole-class or small-group activity.

 ✦ Remind students to use what they already know to make predictions.

Sample Activities

 ✦ Place students in small groups to read a text. Have them use the DRTA strategy to stop at set points during the reading and discuss their predictions. Suggest that students use question words (the 5 Ws and H, pg. 50) as a guide for their discussions.

 ✦ Have students look at the title and illustrations of a text before reading it. Then have students make predictions about what they will read.

Double-Entry Journals

Use this strategy to help students make connections (text-to-text, text-to-self, text-to-world) in texts. Have students create two columns. In the left-hand column, they will document quotations or situations from the text to react to. In the right-hand column, students will record reactions (in the forms of sketches, comments, questions) and form connections after reflecting on their reading.

Ways to Use Double-Entry Journals: during discussions of current events, historical events, biographies, scientific discoveries

Tip for Teaching the Strategy

Provide and post definitions of text-to-text, text-to-self, and text-to-world connections.

Sample Activities

 ✦ Have students trade their journals with partners to share ideas and begin written conversations about what they read.

 ✦ Ask students to share their journals and explain their written responses during a class discussion.

English Language Learner Instruction *(cont.)*
Teaching Strategies *(cont.)*

Echo Reading

Use this strategy to help struggling readers with fluency, pronunciation, intonation, vocabulary, and reading comprehension. The teacher (or other native English speaker) reads the text first, using proper intonation and a good pace. Students follow along silently and then "echo," or imitate, the first reader. Echo reading helps students do the following:

✦ improve sight reading and speaking skills.

✦ build confidence in their pronunciations.

✦ remember important concepts.

Ways to Use Echo Reading: during chants, jingles, songs, poetry, short stories

Tips for Teaching the Strategy

✦ Use gestures to show students which text to read.

✦ Have students who are native English speakers lead the reading; it's helpful for ELLs to hear voices similar to their own.

✦ Adjust the length of text being read to meet the needs of your students. (e.g., For Emerging ELLs, the first reader should read one line of text; for Developing ELLs [and higher levels], the first reader can read several lines of text.)

✦ Adjust tone, pitch, or accent while reading to maintain student interest and engagement.

Sample Activities

✦ Read a short story using echo reading. Have a student who is a native English speaker lead the reading.

✦ Experiment by echoing students on easier parts of a poem or text.

Environmental Print

Use this strategy to connect print materials in home and community settings to those in the classroom. Students read in a known context and add familiar vocabulary. Have students practice the following:

✦ sorting words by categories.

✦ extending vocabulary from a known context to another context.

✦ making connections (pp. 57–59) between environmental print experiences and authentic literature.

Examples: food containers or wrappers, clothing, periodicals, advertisements, street signs

Tips for Teaching the Strategy

✦ Present the concept in a way that acknowledges the age of your students. For example, have students read community fliers from the library.

✦ Use environmental print concepts with word walls or picture glossaries.

Sample Activity

Have each student create a message for another student by cutting out words from magazines and other periodicals. Encourage students to expand their vocabularies and use new words correctly.

GIST (Generating Interactions Between Schemata and Text)

Use this strategy to help students practice summarizing what they have read. Students must read a text, select key ideas (using the 5 Ws and H helps), delete trivial information, and generalize using their own words. They will then shorten their text to 20 words or fewer, with the goal being a concise and precise summary.

Ways to Use GIST: in whole-group or small-group activities; groups can trade lists of words and write summaries using another group's keywords

Tips for Teaching the Strategy

✦ Use with content-area reading.

✦ When used with increasingly large amounts of text, have each student write a GIST for the first section and, after reading the second section, write another GIST that includes the ideas from the second section as well as those from the first GIST.

Sample Activity

Use this strategy as a listening activity. Provide a graphic organizer (see below) or reading guide (pg. 39) for students to follow along and write keywords as they listen. Students will use their notes to write their summaries.

Graphic Organizers

Use this strategy to help students in the following ways:

✦ access background knowledge.

✦ show relationships between new and existing information.

✦ process and organize information while reading.

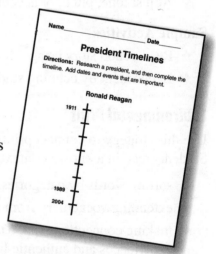

Examples: webs, concept maps, story maps, flow charts, sequence chains, timelines, tables, T-charts, process chart grids or Venn diagrams (use to compare and contrast two or more aspects of something), inquiry charts (provide questions for students to answer using a variety of different sources), observation charts

Tips for Teaching the Strategy

✦ Describe the purpose of the graphic organizer.

✦ Make sure ELLs have the language skills required to complete the organizer.

✦ Simultaneously model and explain completing a sample organizer.

✦ Have students use the graphic organizers independently to complete a task.

✦ Have students generate their own graphic organizers to use within their small groups or to share with other students in the class.

Sample Activity

Prepare an observation chart for students with categories for each of the five senses. Have students observe and explore the topic of study, recording their observations on the chart. For example, students can compare the tastes, textures, etc., of different varieties of apples or other local crops. Students can use their responses to complete a related writing or science activity.

Guided Reading

Use this strategy to help students practice using specific reading strategies. Model reading for students. All students will read the same passage. Have students practice reading the selection with partners and then read it back to a teacher aloud. Support students as they talk about what they have read. Here are the steps to guided reading:

1. Divide students into small groups.
2. Preview a text appropriate to their reading levels. Then read with students using one or more reading strategies.
3. As the students read the text, travel from group to group, providing guidance to individuals based on your observations. (While this interaction takes place, other groups can focus on a literacy activity of your choosing.)
4. After reading, check for understanding by asking questions about the text.

Ways to Use Guided Reading: through stories, short articles, other short passages of informative text; rhyming, rhythmic, or repetitious text

Tips for Teaching the Strategy

✦ Relate guided reading activities to current topics of study in content areas.

✦ Choose to focus on decoding, pronunciation, or grammar skills instead of comprehension skills; use a shared reading activity (pg. 41) to help students focus on meaning.

✦ Have students look for context clues (pg. 71) when they encounter unfamiliar words.

Sample Activity

Select a content-area passage, such as social studies or science, to read with small groups of students. Review the selection to become familiar with insights, humor, and ways to bring the content to life for students. Use guided reading principles and strategies to read and discuss the text. Share interesting background information to help students connect with the text, and encourage them to ask questions and share their insights, as well.

Hands-on Activities

Use this strategy to provide concrete learning experiences for ELLs. Hands-on activities increase students' participation in class by giving them opportunities to practice speaking and listening.

Examples: multisensory explorations, measurement, graphing, construction, models, experiments, mapping, manipulative materials, craft activities, games

Tip for Teaching the Strategy

Provide clear directions and expectations for students at the start of the activity.

Sample Activity

Place several common objects into a backpack or other closed container. Invite a volunteer to come up and secretly take an item out of the container. The student will hide the object so the class cannot see it. That person will then use descriptive words to tell the class about the object while the students try to guess what it is.

Independent Reading

Use this strategy to allow students to practice reading and comprehending text on their own. Help students choose books (appropriate to their reading levels) to read silently.

Examples of Texts to Use With Independent Reading: stories, picture books, nonfiction books, age-appropriate magazines

Tips for Teaching the Strategy

✦ Have students keep reading logs in English or their native languages.

✦ Offer independent reading choices in reading centers with related activities.

✦ Use accelerated reading programs to assess students' reading comprehension.

Sample Activity

Encourage student questioning by asking students to write two or three questions for classmates to answer about an independent reading choice.

Interactive Activities

Use this strategy to increase interactions and allow students extra practice speaking and reading aloud.

Examples: partner reading (pg. 37), student-generated study guides, interviews, games, skits (pg. 42), songs, puppets (provide a safe learning experience for students learning BICS skills)

Tip for Teaching the Strategy

Allow students to see the text of the puppet script to aid in listening comprehension.

Sample Activity

Use one or more common objects. Have students take turns placing the object(s) *in* a box, *under* a book, *over* someone's head, etc., to practice using prepositions. Have a group of students work together and arrange themselves to demonstrate prepositions (e.g., *in front of, behind, next to*).

Jigsaws

Use this strategy to increase student interaction and listening comprehension skills. During a jigsaw, students are given a topic, divided into groups, and assigned individual roles (subtopics). These students then join those who have the same subtopics. After understanding their subtopics, these "specialists" will join their original groups and share their information.

Examples: students hear different excerpts (e.g., podcasts, MP3 technology) and then collaborate to complete questions, students complete charts after reading, students review new vocabulary

Tips for Teaching the Strategy

✦ This activity requires space for groups to meet before the information exchange.

✦ When planning to do a listening jigsaw, consider making your own listening materials. In doing so, you can control the level and content.

Sample Activity

Divide students into groups and then provide them with a text or audio file. Elect group members to evaluate the theme, main characters, plot, setting, conflict, etc., from the story.

English Language Learner Instruction (cont.)
Teaching Strategies (cont.)

K-W-L Charts

Use this strategy to help students activate what they *know* (K), identify what they *want* (W) to learn, and, after learning the concept, discuss what they have *learned* (L).

Ways to Use K-W-L Charts: in pairs, small groups, or as a whole class; pairs share charts with other pairs; small groups share charts with other small groups; individual students illustrate charts or act out concepts to the class

Tips for Teaching the Strategy

✦ Refer to previous classroom concepts to get students thinking about what they already know.

✦ Encourage students to make connections.

✦ Invite students to explore their curiosity about a topic.

✦ After reading, have students check and correct any misconceptions in the "K" column.

Sample Activity

Have students complete the first column of the K-W-L chart individually. Then ask them to trade charts with partners. Have the partner introduce what the other partner (Kwan) knows about the solar system. "Kwan knows that the solar system has more than one dwarf planet." Have students complete the second column of their charts on their own. Students will trade with a different partner (Takira) to highlight classmates' thinking. "Takira wants to learn if life could exist on other planets in the solar system." After students have completed the "L" column of the chart, have them tell partners what they have learned.

K-W-L Chart Variations

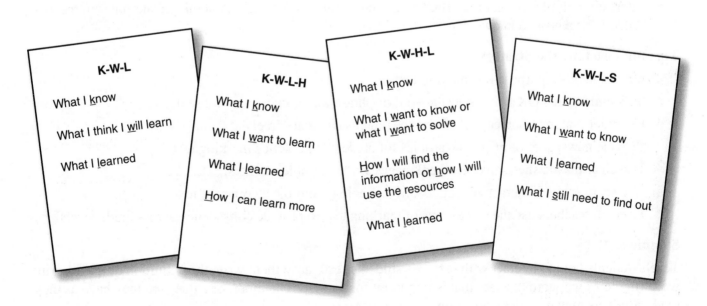

K-W-L

What I know

What I think I will learn

What I learned

K-W-L-H

What I know

What I want to learn

What I learned

How I can learn more

K-W-H-L

What I know

What I want to know or what I want to solve

How I will find the information or how I will use the resources

What I learned

K-W-L-S

What I know

What I want to know

What I learned

What I still need to find out

Marking Text

Use this strategy to teach students how to mark text, or make notations, as they read. Marking text allows students to interact with what they read, increasing their comprehension. This strategy helps students to do the following:

- ◆ comprehend what they read.
- ◆ notice and learn patterns of language.
- ◆ identify the main idea and details.
- ◆ remember what they thought about the text.

Examples

- ◆ underlining or circling keywords or phrases
- ◆ circling specific vocabulary words and defining them in the margins
- ◆ identifying and numbering examples
- ◆ writing the main idea in the margins
- ◆ writing questions at the top of the page to ask in class
- ◆ writing a one-sentence summary at the end of each page or section

- ◆ using sticky notes to mark text or pages
- ◆ using colors to identify parts of speech
- ◆ developing letters or symbols to code markings, for example, a "?" for a question, a star for an interesting bit of information, "BK" or another symbol to indicate something that relates to the reader's background knowledge

Tips for Teaching the Strategy

- ◆ Give students a purpose for marking text.
- ◆ Tell students it's OK to mark just a word or phrase rather than an entire sentence.
- ◆ Consider making photocopies of text so students can mark freely.
- ◆ Provide newspaper or magazine articles for students to practice marking text.
- ◆ Use clear plastic sheets over textbook pages with washable markers.
- ◆ Use scanners and interactive whiteboard technology to project copies of text.
- ◆ Have all teachers use the same ways of marking text to provide consistency across grade levels.

Sample Activity

Teach students how to interact with text. As students read, have them write the definition of a bold-print word (in their own words), a fact that is important for them to remember, or a question they have as they read. Students may use sticky notes for this exercise.

Modeling

Use this strategy to model, or show by example, how to do something. Modeling provides students with a pattern or guideline to follow and implement in their own learning.

Ways to Use Modeling: through reading strategies, writing techniques, language structures, completing tasks, expectations for classroom behavior, student work

Tips for Teaching the Strategy

+ Set an example and read silently at least one day a week when students read during independent reading time.
+ Talk about your own reading or writing with the class.

Sample Activity

Model for students how to set up and complete a science experiment.

Oral Reading

Use this strategy to give students repeated opportunities to practice decoding and reading text. Model oral reading for students first. Other students may also model oral reading, especially for ELLs still in the silent phase. (ELLs may use gestures to start.)

Ways to Use Oral Reading: through target word cards, wordless picture books, environmental print (pg. 31), simple narrative text

Tips for Teaching the Strategy

+ Have students use puppets to read simple text.
+ Use this strategy with group activities.

Sample Activity

Have students practice reading aloud by reading something they have written for a presentation. Students may practice with partners or in small groups before reading in front of the whole class to improve fluency and decrease dependence on their written notes.

Partner Reading

Use this strategy to give students more independent practice reading aloud. Model how to take turns reading, how to help a partner self-correct, and how to ask a partner questions. Have students take turns reading with partners.

Ways to Pair Students: by similar ability, by language proficiency level (e.g., Expanding and Bridging learners can provide support for Entering and Beginning learners.), by native language (bilingual support for clarification)

Tips for Teaching the Strategy

+ Have students divide the reading, or assign reading passages to students.
+ Use partner reading to support students when they read textbooks.

Sample Activity

Have students write their own pieces. A partner will read the written piece back to the student who wrote the piece. This strategy may also help students edit their own writing.

English Language Learner Instruction (cont.)
Teaching Strategies (cont.)

Peer Tutoring

Use this strategy to train students in instructional methods so they can help one another. Both partners benefit; sometimes, the tutors gain more than the recipients. Consider selecting tutors based on who needs to gain which skills. Give all students opportunities to participate as tutors.

Examples: Discuss learning, ask and respond to questions (pg. 50), correct work, provide and receive feedback, etc.

Tips for Teaching the Strategy

✦ Establish procedures for forming tutoring pairs or groups quickly and quietly.

✦ Use materials that match students' levels of ability.

✦ Teach desired behaviors, such as respect and calm acceptance upon receiving feedback for incorrect answers.

✦ Provide a structure for tutoring sessions and a way for students to track their progress.

✦ Consider rewards for students who stay on task.

Sample Activity

Pair a student who does well academically with a student who needs assistance. Have the pair discuss topics of interest, particularly for the lower-achieving student. Encourage students to form a friendly working relationship, in which both members of the pair can contribute.

Read-Alouds

Use this strategy to have students set a purpose for reading and to listen based on that purpose. During read-alouds, the teacher or student(s) reads aloud a passage or story while others listen. Here are the steps to a read-aloud:

1. Choose a book that addresses the reading levels of your students, and read it aloud.
2. Model a specific reading strategy for each lesson.
3. Pose questions for students to think about as they listen.
4. Throughout the read-aloud, have students make predictions, check their predictions, and make new predictions.

Examples of Read-Aloud Materials: word cards, magazine articles, textbooks, text on charts, interactive whiteboard files

Tips for Teaching the Strategy

✦ Use a read-aloud experience to introduce a lesson concept.

✦ Combine a read-aloud with a think-aloud (pg. 43) to help students interact with what they hear read aloud.

✦ Provide visual aids (pg. 44) to help students learn new vocabulary.

Sample Activity

Use a read-aloud to introduce a novel and demonstrate how to think about what is read. Read a few pages of the novel and pause to discuss. Have students ask questions and clarify words and concepts as needed. Continue reading and discussing until the end of a section or chapter, inviting students to read along silently as you read aloud.

Reading Guides

Use this strategy to identify the levels of comprehension in students. These teacher-created guides help alert students to text features and other information as they read assigned texts.

Examples: story maps or other graphic organizers (pg. 32), discussion questions to answer, guidelines to mark text (pg. 36), a list of question words (5 Ws and H)

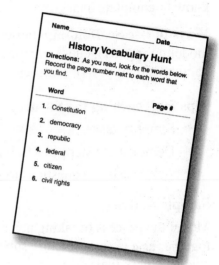

Tips for Teaching the Strategy

✦ Reading guides may be used as listening guides for a read-aloud (pg. 38) or content-area video.

✦ Give students hand motions to use when they hear specific words or phrases in a story; use movement as a listening guide.

Sample Activity

Provide a list of vocabulary words or specific facts, phrases, or other information for students to find as they read. Have them note the page number on which they read each piece of information.

Reciprocal Teaching

Use this strategy to help students construct meaning and set a purpose for reading. Using dialogue, the teacher and students will take turns summarizing, generating questions, clarifying, and predicting.

Examples: teacher role reversal, groups with assigned roles, individuals with assigned roles who meet in groups to compare notes, peer tutoring (pg. 38), cooperative groups (pg. 28), jigsaws (pg. 34)

Tips for Teaching the Strategy

✦ Use a template or other graphic organizer (pg. 32) to guide students through the process.

✦ Guide discussion as needed.

✦ Break text into smaller "chunks."

✦ Monitor student responses and check for comprehension.

Sample Activity

Have students create charts incorporating the four aspects of reciprocal teaching: summarizing (pg. 65), generating questions (pg. 50), clarifying (pg. 52), and predicting (pp. 62–63). Then have students use the charts to guide their thinking in small-group discussions.

English Language Learner Instruction (cont.)
Teaching Strategies (cont.)

Scaffolding

Use this strategy to help students complete tasks while encouraging them to do as much as they can on their own. Scaffolding acts as a bridge between what the student knows and what the student needs to know to complete a task.

Ways to Use Scaffolding: through visual aids (pg. 44), manipulative materials, realia, examples, modeling (pg. 37), cues, prompts, hints, partial solutions, lists, tables, graphs, think-alouds (pg. 43), paraphrasing (pg. 64), sentence frames (pg. 40)

Tips for Teaching the Strategy

✦ Simplify tasks.

✦ Demonstrate steps in a task.

✦ Ask a series of questions to scaffold students during a class discussion.

Sample Activity

Model the process of taking notes for a writing task. Then have students read and take notes. Work together as a class to identify subcategories for the main topic. Assign each subtopic a color, and have students mark their notes accordingly. Students may also use scissors to cut out and rearrange sentence strips in a logical order. Students can use their notes and sentence strips to write rough drafts.

Sentence Frames

Use this strategy to provide structure for students learning academic language. This strategy gives students phrases that they can complete. Use sentence frames to do the following:

✦ have students complete written work in an activity.

✦ help students learn grammatical structure.

✦ support students when they write responses.

✦ help students make connections to prior learning, make predictions, or compare and contrast.

Examples: "I predict that _____"; "While reading, I used the strategy to _____"; "My conclusion is _____ because _____."

Tip for Teaching the Strategy

Sentence difficulty should depend on language level. Use simple sentence frames for Entering ELLs, comparative sentence frames for Developing ELLs, and complex-comparative sentence frames for Bridging ELLs.

Sample Activity

Write sentence frames on sentence strips or use them with an interactive whiteboard.

English Language Learner Instruction *(cont.)*
Teaching Strategies *(cont.)*

Sentence Patterning

Use this strategy to help students become familiar with sentence patterns. By recognizing basic types of sentence structures in English, students are developing their reading and writing skills. Sentence patterning helps students understand parts of speech and verb tenses.

Ways to Use Sentence Patterning: through chants, cloze activities (pg. 28), sentence charts

Tips for Teaching the Strategy

- Have students practice using different verb tenses.
- Allow students to get creative in their adjective use.
- Expand with locations and adverbs.
- Point out the use of articles in English as needed.

Sample Activity

Have students participate in creating a class chart, such as the one on the right, to display basic English sentence structures.

Basic Sentence Structures	
Subject – Verb	Hasina reads.
Subject – Verb – Object	Miguel likes birds.
Subject – Verb – Adjective	Anton is happy.
Subject – Verb – Adverb	Amaya swims fast.
Subject – Verb – (Article –) Noun	Kai kicked the ball.

Shared Reading

Use this strategy to encourage students to connect with, anticipate, and make predictions about a text. Shared reading supports readers as they begin to understand details in texts while still focusing on meaning and enjoying what is being read. Shared reading may incorporate another reading strategy, such as echo reading (pg. 31) or choral reading (pg. 27). Here are the steps to this strategy:

1. Preview the text before reading—ask questions and use the text's illustrations to elicit responses and predictions.
2. As you read, check students' predictions against the text of the story.
3. Re-read the book over several days, focusing on a different aspect each time. For example, you may ask students to look for high-frequency, rhyming, or multisyllabic words.
4. Discuss the text after each reading.

Ways to Use Shared Reading: during stories, expository text, poetry, songs

Tips for Teaching the Strategy

- Introduce students to text slightly above their comfort reading levels.
- Use materials on a subject with which students are unfamiliar. Demonstrate how students can learn through reading, for example, how to bake bread.
- Use an overhead projector or interactive whiteboard to make text visible to all students.

Sample Activity

Incorporate quick activities during a shared reading experience, such as having students skim a paragraph to find a specific fact, describe the connection between a caption and photograph, etc.

English Language Learner Instruction *(cont.)*
Teaching Strategies *(cont.)*

Simulations

Use this strategy when real-life processes happen too quickly to study, take too long, or are too dangerous, expensive, or inaccessible.

Examples: role-play, computer simulations (virtual reality), drama, modeling (pg. 37), games, cartoon drawings, books (e.g., *Choose Your Own Adventure*), interactive whiteboard software

Tips for Teaching the Strategy

✦ Explain all the parts of an activity (using visual aids, if needed) before starting.

✦ Give students role cards as needed.

Sample Activity

When studying a particular migration group, students can imagine weather and other travel conditions to determine what the people would encounter and need for the journeys.

Skits / Readers' Theater

Use this strategy to give students extra practice before reading aloud in front of the class. Have students practice reading the lines for their roles from a script. Allow students enough time to read their lines multiple times before reading in front of others.

Examples: plays, skits, readers' theater scripts (available from online resources), simple stories rewritten as scripts

Tips for Teaching the Strategy

✦ Have some props available and allow students to use them.

✦ Encourage students to sit in chairs or stand in front of the class to help others hear better.

✦ Provide stands for scripts. Show students how to read and look over the stand towards the audience. Explain that this keeps readers' voices from being muffled and makes it easier for others to hear them read.

✦ Rewrite portions of content-area text or have students assist in writing fiction or nonfiction texts.

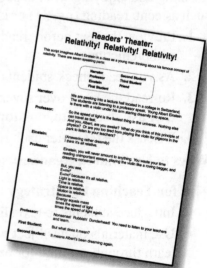

Sample Activity

Have students read the roles of characters in a popular comic strip.

Think-Alouds

Use this strategy to model thought processes while reading, writing, or demonstrating an activity to students. In doing so, you are showing your problem-solving techniques, which students can reflect on and adopt as their own. Think-alouds also demonstrate to students that they are not alone in having to think their way through tasks. Here are the basic steps to a think-aloud:

1. Choose a book and read it out loud.
2. Stop to make comments while reading.
3. Have students discuss what they observed while you were thinking aloud.

Alternatively, you can modify the steps using one or several of the following options:

✦ Continue reading, allowing students to stop you at any time and ask what you are thinking.

✦ Reverse the process. Call on a volunteer during whole-class reading, and ask that student what he or she is thinking as he or she reads.

✦ Have students practice with partners or in small groups.

✦ Have students write their own think-aloud statements. (e.g., "This makes me think that . . . ," "I don't understand _____, so I'll . . .")

Ways to Use Think-Alouds: when comparing and contrasting (pg. 53), practicing cause and effect, analyzing specific plot events, discussing word patterns

Tips for Teaching the Strategy

✦ Pre-read and place sticky notes to remind yourself of your thoughts as you read.

✦ Plan ahead when to stop and think aloud.

Sample Activity

Model a think-aloud by reading a poem. Invite students to think aloud with you during a second reading of the poem. Give students phrases such as, "I picture . . . ," "I wonder . . . ," etc.

Think-Pair-Share

Use this strategy so ELLs can rehearse what they want to say, negotiate meaning with partners, and expand or correct their understanding. Here are the steps to think-pair-share:

1. Ask a question.
2. Have students think for a moment silently.
3. Ask students to share their ideas with partners.
4. Call on volunteers to share with the class.

Ways to Use Think-Pair-Share: during class discussions; brainstorming (pg. 27); story, reading passage, or textbook questions; science activities

Tips for Teaching the Strategy

✦ Have students turn in their notes to check for gaps in understanding.

✦ Listen carefully to ELLs as they discuss with partners.

Sample Activity

Have students discuss characters or plot in a narrative story.

English Language Learner Instruction *(cont.)*
Teaching Strategies *(cont.)*

TPR (Total Physical Response)

Use this strategy to incorporate physical movements, as well as the sounds, words, or phrases associated with these movements, into your lessons. Using TPR, students respond physically to commands or statements made by the teacher (e.g., "stand up," "sit down," "jump"). The physical response demonstrates understanding.

Examples: looking at a picture; pointing to a picture, object, or word; gestures to express "yes" or "no" to simple questions; a series of body movements to learn a series of sounds or words

Tips for Teaching the Strategy

✦ Keep movements and related words consistent.

✦ Connect specific gestures with phonics or target words.

Sample Activity

Have students read a page from a story. Select a student at random to act out one thing a character did in the story. If other students agree that the character did that action, they copy the movement. Invite other students to add subsequent actions expressed in the story. Have students provide phrases or sentences (depending on language level) that describe the action.

Visual Aids

Use this strategy to help those who are visual learners "see" what they need to know. Visual aids do not rely on as much written or spoken language as texts do to communicate concepts. Use visual aids to help students clarify meaning and relate new vocabulary and concepts to visual images.

Examples: realia, drawings, diagrams, graphs, lists, charts, posters, maps, overhead transparencies, slide shows, videos, illustrated books, photographs, interactive whiteboard

Tips for Teaching the Strategy

✦ Reproduce copies of lessons for ELLs, if possible.

✦ Use different colors to relate to key points.

Sample Activity

Have students read social studies texts with pictures. Use the pictures as visual aids to help students retell what they have read.

Whole-Group Response

Use this strategy to help students lower their anxiety and gain confidence when providing answers. Because students are not singled out to give responses, they feel more comfortable sharing. For this reason, more students maintain focus and want to respond.

Examples: Have students point to something, raise their hands or fingers, answer in chorus (pg. 27), use body movements or gestures, check off items on a list, say chants with motions, etc.

Tip for Teaching the Strategy

Engage students by matching a type of whole-group response to their interests, for example, a popular tune from a commercial with the words rewritten to practice academic concepts.

Sample Activity

Invite students to create a chant or choral response to review a social studies lesson. Students can take turns being the "leader" in the chant or choral reading (pg. 27).

English Language Learner Instruction *(cont.)*
Strategies Across the Content Areas

Many teaching strategies can be implemented in more than one content area. Use the page numbers to refer back to individual strategies for examples and ideas to adapt a strategy to teach specific content.

Strategy	Reading	Writing	Social Studies	Science
Brainstorming (pg. 27)		X	X	X
Choral Reading (pg. 27)	X		X	X
Cloze Activities (pg. 28)	X	X	X	X
Cooperative Groups (pg. 28)	X	X	X	X
Dialogue Journals (pg. 29)	X	X	X	X
DLTA (pg. 29)	X		X	X
DRTA (pg. 30)	X		X	X
Double-Entry Journals (pg. 30)	X	X	X	X
Echo Reading (pg. 31)	X		X	X
Environmental Print (pg. 31)	X	X	X	X
GIST (pg. 32)	X	X	X	X
Graphic Organizers (pg. 32)	X	X	X	X
Guided Reading (pg. 33)	X		X	X
Hands-on Activities (pg. 33)		X	X	X
Independent Reading (pg. 34)	X		X	X
Interactive Activities (pg. 34)	X		X	X
Jigsaws (pg. 34)	X		X	X
K-W-L Charts (pg. 35)	X	X	X	X
Marking Text (pg. 36)	X	X	X	X
Modeling (pg. 37)	X	X	X	X
Oral Reading (pg. 37)	X		X	X

English Language Learner Instruction (cont.)
Strategies Across the Content Areas (cont.)

Strategy	Reading	Writing	Social Studies	Science
Partner Reading (pg. 37)	X	X	X	X
Peer Tutoring (pg. 38)	X	X	X	X
Read-Alouds (pg. 38)	X		X	X
Reading Guides (pg. 39)	X	X	X	X
Reciprocal Teaching (pg. 39)	X		X	X
Scaffolding (pg. 40)	X	X	X	X
Sentence Frames (pg. 40)	X	X	X	X
Sentence Patterning (pg. 41)	X	X	X	X
Shared Reading (pg. 41)	X		X	X
Simulations (pg. 42)	X		X	X
Skits / Readers' Theater (pg. 42)	X	X	X	X
Think-Alouds (pg. 43)	X	X	X	X
Think-Pair-Share (pg. 43)	X	X	X	X
TPR (pg. 44)	X		X	X
Visual Aids (pg. 44)	X		X	X
Whole-Group Response (pg. 44)	X		X	X

Student Literacy Connections
Understanding Literacy

Literacy refers to the ability to read and write. In a broader sense, it encompasses learning, or making sense out of new information. What we already know determines how we construct meaning from what we read, which helps us to understand the world in which we live.

Literacy is affected by various factors, including family and home environments, music, traditions, technology, etc. As a teacher, it's important to recognize these factors and create a classroom environment that encourages literacy. Consider sharing your individual or family literacy with students by bringing in printed materials from home. Invite students to reciprocate so that you can learn as much as possible about each student's abilities in English.

Increasing literacy is a joint venture. While it's important for teachers to implement teaching strategies, it's just as important for students to adopt some of their own. The following pages include teacher tips for literacy, actions to improve reading comprehension, and strategies for students. Model and teach these strategies to students. Suggest that when they have trouble understanding what they read, they try one of them.

Additionally, the tips below can aid students in monitoring their own comprehension. Consider photocopying and enlarging this list for classroom display.

Student Tips for Literacy

- ✦ Talk through the thinking and reading process using the following sentence frames:

    - I know _____ (title) takes place_____.

    - I already know _____ about _____ (topic).

    - When I think about the setting, I realize that _____.

    - I can use _____ (new information) to _____.

- ✦ Pause and check for understanding.

- ✦ Re-read a passage if necessary.

- ✦ Read quietly to yourself to focus on, understand, and remember what you read.

- ✦ Read aloud with a partner to help you understand.

- ✦ Repeat what you have read to yourself.

- ✦ Tell someone else what you have read.

- ✦ Determine word meanings.

- ✦ Cover up a word that you don't know and try a word that you do know in its place to learn what the new word means.

- ✦ Ask questions as you read.

- ✦ Make predictions. Then check and revise them.

- ✦ Monitor your comprehension and adjust how you read to improve your understanding.

Teacher Tips for Literacy

✦ Model enjoyment and comprehension of reading.

✦ Use big books (especially nonfiction) to engage students in illustrations and text.

✦ Demonstrate different teaching and student strategies using a variety of texts.

✦ Focus on only one strategy during a reading conference or lesson.

✦ Provide reading experiences for students to help them develop meaning.

✦ When showing videos in class, use the closed-captioning feature so that students can match spoken and written language.

✦ Allow students to practice reading a section of text before you read it aloud in front of the class.

✦ Check to see if students express confusion or understanding.

✦ Give students opportunities to express their opinions about texts both orally and in writing.

✦ Teach phonetic skills.

✦ Teach the differences between various forms of written and oral language (BICS and CALP): blogging, texting, email, informal speech, classroom speech, and academic language.

✦ Preteach vocabulary for specific reading skills.

✦ Teach students to notice typographic cues, such as punctuation marks.

✦ Explain the various purposes of reading:

- to share information

- to gain new knowledge

- to form an opinion

- to learn how to do something

- to experience and enjoy stories

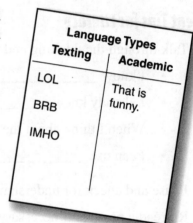

| Language Types | |
Texting	Academic
LOL	That is funny.
BRB	
IMHO	

Student Literacy Connections (cont.)
Actions to Improve Reading Comprehension

The chart below includes actions that teachers and students can perform in order to improve students' overall reading comprehension.

Teacher Actions	Student Actions
Read aloud every day.	Read every day.
Offer a variety of reading choices at or slightly above students' levels.	Read across the content areas.
Implement and model teaching strategies (pp. 27–44).	Re-read familiar texts to improve literacy skills and comprehension.
Teach students how to use student strategies (pp. 50–72).	Give a variety of responses to reading: oral, written, and artistic.
Focus on and review key concepts from texts.	Learn and use student strategies (pp. 50–72).
Explain language and content as needed to build on prior knowledge.	Discuss texts in your native language if another student speaks the same language.
Rewrite passages to break long, complicated sentences into short, simplified sentences.	Help classmates with understanding words and phrases when discussing text in a small group.
Help students recognize any cognates or other similarities between their native languages and English.	Write responses to reading in your native language and turn them in. (Translation resources can be used.)
Use motions, gestures, and visual aids to anchor meaning.	Ask questions about the text.
Ask questions to engage students in direct conversation about reading.	Analyze how the title, headings, and illustrations relate to the text.
Use texts with familiar vocabulary.	Follow a reading guide.
Use games and interactive whiteboard activities to develop reading and listening comprehension.	Mark text or use sticky notes to identify purposes for reading.
Provide various writing exercises to allow students to interact with text.	Practice sequencing the events of a story by sketching picture cards or rewriting sentences in the proper order.
Provide examples to show students how to interact effectively with expository text.	
Teach students to monitor their comprehension.	

Student Literacy Connections *(cont.)*
Strategies for Students

Asking Questions

Question words help students identify specific information. Students can ask questions about people, places, events, things, quantities, or characteristics. Asking questions helps students interact with text and apply what they learn. Students can ask questions to identify and remember what is important in a selection. They can also use questions to check how well they understand text.

Tips for Teaching the Strategy

✦ Teach the question words: *who, what, where, when, why,* and *how.*

✦ Consider introducing the question words using students' native languages.

✦ Begin by having students ask each other questions in conversation, and then transfer the skill to academic tasks.

✦ Use objects as you ask questions to engage students.

✦ Use sentence frames (pg. 40) to help students answer questions, such as these:

- When you said _____, did you mean _____?
- I know _____ because it says _____ in the text.
- I came to the conclusion that _____ because _____.
- If _____ happened, then _____.

✦ Teach students how word order changes when asking a question. Give examples.

	Across the Content Areas
Reading	Use questions to preview text features, including the title, chapters, headings, and visual information. Have students use sticky notes to write questions as they read. Invite students to share their questions with partners or the whole class to begin a discussion about the reading. Have students ask each other questions about stories during independent reading time.
Writing	Have students use double-entry journals (pg. 30) with questions in one column and answers or further related questions in the second column. Students may trade their journals with partners to begin written conversations about what they read. Invite students to write letters containing questions to the author of the book they're reading.
Social Studies	Set up a question tree using a simple hierarchy diagram or a pictorial representation of a tree with branches. Begin with students' questions prior to a social studies reading. Add answers as they read. Encourage students to write further questions as they read and add those to the tree. Use the skill of asking questions to help students think as they read.
Science	Help students understand the problem-solving process by giving them questions, such as "What is the question?" "Where/How can I find the information I need?" and "How will I solve this problem?" Develop students' observation skills by playing a game using science questions, such as a version of "20 Questions," "Jeopardy!" or "I Spy."

Building Background Knowledge

Students build background knowledge when they can relate what they learn in class to something they already know. Teachers help students develop this skill by being aware of how topics connect to their students' lives. It also helps to evaluate or assess students' prior knowledge about a topic before teaching.

Tips for Teaching the Strategy

✦ Relate new concepts to students' personal experiences.

✦ Help students connect new ideas to what they already know.

✦ Consider how the following relate to your students:

- cultural backgrounds
- previous educational experiences
- customs and traditions
- music and art
- historical figures
- geography

Independence Days

U.S.—July 4
India—August 15
Mexico—September 16

✦ Encourage students to draw on their cultural experiences to contribute to class discussions.

✦ Have students talk with family members to learn their views on a particular topic.

✦ Teach culture-specific background information as needed.

✦ Model with a think-aloud (pg. 43).

Across the Content Areas	
Reading	Provide students with a brief prompt to discuss prior to reading or viewing lesson content. Have students complete a specific task related to the topic to access background knowledge. For example, if students read a selection about food or cooking, have them turn and share favorite family recipes with partners.
Writing	Have students use brainstorming techniques (pg. 27). Have students use graphic organizers (pg. 32).
Social Studies	Read aloud a social studies text to have students start thinking about the topic. Ask students to complete a sentence frame (pg. 40), such as "I can use _____ (new information) to _____."
Science	Have students use K-W-L charts and variations (pg. 35) during a science lesson. Have students interview partners about the topic being studied and share their interview results with the class.

Clarifying

When students have trouble understanding the events in a reading selection, teach them to clarify meaning to increase reading comprehension. Students can re-read, look for visual cues, check the pronunciation of a word they don't know, or read the context to determine the meaning of a new word. It's important that ELLs stop and clarify when they read something they don't understand.

Tips for Teaching the Strategy

✦ Use native language materials to explain new words and concepts.

✦ Allow students to ask for clarification in their native languages (orally or in writing); use translation resources to translate.

✦ Have students write notes to clarify meaning.

✦ Teach students to look for textual cues, such as punctuation or font characteristics.

✦ Help students use word study skills, such as the following:

- looking for little words inside big words.
- noticing prefixes and suffixes.
- noticing compound words.
- identifying root words and cognates.
- understanding and using synonyms and antonyms.

✦ Encourage students to ask other students in their groups for help.

✦ Use evidence and give examples to show students how to clarify meaning as they read.

Across the Content Areas	
Reading	Have students mark unknown words (pg. 36) with sticky notes so they can look them up in a dictionary later.
	Remind them to ask questions, such as "What clues will help me understand what I'm reading?"
	Help students understand story characters by asking about the feelings, moods, and actions of the characters.
Writing	Have students map out (written or pictorial) a story before they write.
Social Studies	Cover up one or more words so students can substitute similar words that make sense in the context to learn meanings.
	Encourage students to use visualization techniques (pg. 72) when they don't understand their social studies text.
Science	Have students create their own cloze exercises (pg. 28) with unfamiliar science reading passages.
	Have students guess the meaning of a new science word, check with partners, and then use a dictionary to confirm.
	Give students strategies to clarify as they read, such as re-reading text, asking questions, and thinking aloud.

Comparing and Contrasting

We compare when we look for ways in which things are alike. We contrast when we look for ways in which things are different. When students are comparing and contrasting, they are grouping ideas into categories, noticing clues in the text, and clarifying their thinking.

Tips for Teaching the Strategy

✦ Teach the meanings of *compare* and *contrast*, and introduce students to some of the most common signal words.

- *Compare:* in comparison, at the same time, like, both, similarly
- *Contrast:* however, but, yet, in contrast, compared with, different from, unlike

✦ Help students determine what to compare and contrast before they read.

✦ Allow students to compare and/or contrast one text to another text or a text to their personal knowledge, opinions, and beliefs.

✦ Have students mark text (pg. 36), using one color to compare and a different color to contrast.

✦ Have students use a T-chart or Venn diagram to compare and contrast (pg. 32).

✦ Introduce similes as a way to compare things in writing. Similes are phrases that use the words *like* or *as* to compare two unlike things. For example, "He falls like a thunderbolt."

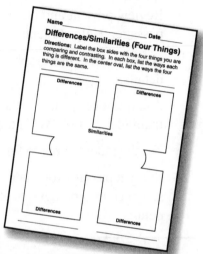

Across the Content Areas	
Reading	Have students compare and/or contrast two texts. Have students focus on one specific aspect of a story, such as a character, to compare or contrast with another. Show students examples in which an author compares and contrasts two or more things. Discuss how the things are similar and different.
Writing	Have students discuss or reflect on their comparisons and make relevant connections to their learning in a writing assignment. Have students discuss with partners and then write journal entries to summarize their comparisons.
Social Studies	Have students compare and contrast their opinions with those of an author in debate form, with one side taking the author's perspective and the other side taking the students' perspectives.
Science	Use Venn diagrams, T-charts, or other types of charts and tables. Have students compare their previous knowledge with what they learned from the science text.

Student Literacy Connections (cont.)
Strategies for Students (cont.)

Finding Main Ideas and Details

Identifying important information in a text will help students determine the main idea, or what the passage is about. Students should be able to state the main idea in one or two sentences. Details that go with the main idea relate specifically to it and give more information about what is happening.

Tips for Teaching the Strategy

✦ Teach the question words used to find details in a text: *who, what, where, when, why,* and *how.*

✦ Start with shorter passages to have students identify the main idea and details before working with a whole story.

✦ Review present and past tense so students can use the correct tense when reflecting on a reading passage. Help students answer reading questions using the correct tenses.

✦ Have students use graphic organizers (pg. 32), such as an outline, to identify the main idea and details.

✦ Ask questions, such as these: "What is this passage about?" "What details help me understand the main idea?" and "What did I learn?"

✦ Teach students how to find keywords.

✦ Study a passage together. Ask students to locate where they found the main idea (e.g., the topic sentence of a paragraph, at the end of the section). Model how to mark text (pg. 36) to identify details.

Across the Content Areas	
Reading	Provide each student with a picture and a sentence that may describe the picture's main idea. Begin by telling a student who has a matching sentence and picture to go to one side and a student who has a sentence and picture that do not match to go to the other side. Continue with a few more examples and then challenge students to try to place themselves accurately. Review the matches, allowing students to share the sentences they're holding.
Writing	Divide students into groups and give each group a picture. Have the group work together to create one sentence that describes what the picture is about. Then have students list details that relate to the main idea of the picture. Have groups take turns sharing their sentences and word lists with the class without showing their pictures. Class members will draw pictures based on the descriptions. Compare student drawings with the actual pictures.
Social Studies	Have students sort social studies examples into "main idea" and "details" categories on a T-chart.
Science	Have students independently take notes about the details of a science passage and then determine the main idea in small-group discussions.

Identifying Facts and Opinions

Facts are true and real; they can be proven true or false. Opinions express personal thoughts, feelings, and favorites. They are not the same for everyone. Texts often contain facts as well as opinions. When students learn the difference between the two, it helps them to understand what they read, sort information, and evaluate what they learn.

Tips for Teaching the Strategy

✦ Explain that it is possible to look up factual information to find out if it is true or false.

✦ Teach keywords that indicate opinions, such as *think, feel, most, least, best, worst, always, never,* and *believe*; opinions have descriptive words.

✦ Remind students that texts and webpages often mix fact and opinion together, and they need to be able to tell the difference.

✦ Model a think-aloud (pg. 43) for processing facts and opinions. For example, "When my friend tells me about something he heard or read, I always ask him where he got the information."

✦ Give students examples of facts and opinions in a sample passage, TV commercial, or magazine advertisement.

✦ Have students create their own fact/opinion charts based on "What I think" and "What I know."

✦ Discuss the concept that it's OK for one person to think one thing and for someone else to think something different about the same topic as long as everyone recognizes that these are opinions.

Across the Content Areas	
Reading	Read a passage together as a class. Use one color to underline words or phrases that indicate a fact and another color to underline words or phrases that indicate an opinion.
Writing	Have students write fact or opinion statements on cards. Classmates will guess which type of statement it is. Invite students to try to trick one another.
	Group students in pairs. Say a word aloud for the whole class. One partner in each pair will write a fact about the word, and the other partner will write an opinion about the word.
Social Studies	Create a T-chart for a social studies passage or topic. List opinions on one side under "What I Think" and facts on the other side under "What I Know."
	Have students participate in a sorting game with social studies fact-and-opinion sentence strips.
Science	Have students state facts and opinions about several different science objects. Then follow up with a discussion about attributes of objects.
	Give each student one index card. Have students write the word *fact* on one side of the cards and the word *opinion* on the other side. Read science statements aloud. Students will show the correct side of their cards.

Student Literacy Connections *(cont.)*
Strategies for Students *(cont.)*

Listening

Listening helps ELLs become familiar with the sounds, patterns, and rhythms of English. Provide students with many opportunities to listen to a variety of materials in different settings and contexts.

Tips for Teaching the Strategy

✦ Help students distinguish between similar sounds in English.

✦ Have students listen, observe, and participate to learn new vocabulary.

✦ Help students learn word meanings with repeated readings.

✦ Give students opportunities to listen to words and phrases in multiple contexts.

✦ Inform students that they can track with a finger or other small pointer to follow along as they listen to fiction and nonfiction text.

✦ Use an anticipation guide to prepare students to listen with greater comprehension. For example, read a list of statements related to the reading, and ask students to demonstrate with a thumbs-up or thumbs-down whether they agree with each statement. Alternatively, students may check written statements or complete another type of graphic organizer, such as a T-chart, prior to listening to preview the material.

✦ Have students play a listening game related to a particular topic of study. Read a passage with action cues or hand motions to help students follow along as they listen.

✦ Check with local media centers (school or community libraries) to obtain recordings on various topics.

Across the Content Areas	
Reading	Have students learn new vocabulary by listening to prerecorded songs. First, write the new vocabulary words on cards. Then place these cards on the board. Target and introduce new vocabulary before students listen to the song. After they hear the song once, divide the class into two teams and assign a letter or number to each team (e.g., A, B; 1, 2). As they hear targeted words in the song, students from each team will take turns going to the board and writing their team's letter or number on the vocabulary cards.
Writing	Have students participate in class listening activities, such as debates or skits (pg. 42). Encourage students to write their own scripts.
Social Studies	Download social studies-related recordings for students to play using MP3 or computer technology.
Science	Have students watch science video clips with or without the closed-captioning feature.

Student Literacy Connections (cont.)
Strategies for Students (cont.)

Making Connections

Students make connections to what they read when they relate it to their lives, other texts, or the world. They may read a passage that reminds them of something that happened to them in the past. Or the text may remind them of things they have already read. Or perhaps the text reminds them of a particular place or event. Help students make the following connections: text-to-self, text-to-text, and text-to-world. As a class, determine symbols that students can use to identify the connections as they read.

Tips for Teaching the Strategy

Text-to-Self

  ✦ Encourage students to think about how they feel when they read a passage.

  ✦ Have students highlight their favorite parts of a passage and tell how they can relate to it.

  ✦ Discuss similarities between the selection and students' prior knowledge or experiences.

  ✦ Model a think-aloud (pg. 43), demonstrating how to relate text to something you have previously experienced, read, or learned.

  ✦ Have students use graphic organizers (pg. 32) to help them make connections.

Text-to-Text

  ✦ Discuss with students other texts (including TV shows, movies, games, stories, nonfiction books) that the selection reminds them of.

  ✦ Discuss similarities between texts as a class.

  ✦ Have students use journals to cross-reference related texts.

  ✦ Have students complete Venn diagrams or T-charts to compare texts to other stories, books, songs, or movies.

Text-to-World

  ✦ Use pictures, visual representations, or actual objects to show connections.

  ✦ Ask questions or give examples to show students how an event in a story relates to something that happens in everyday life.

  ✦ Model making connections between text and something students may have encountered in the media (TV, newspapers, magazines, advertisements).

  ✦ Give students prompts, such as "This reminds me of the real world because . . ."

  ✦ Use maps to help students identify places mentioned in texts.

Making Connections *(cont.)*

Use Multimedia to Make Text-to-World Connections

Multimedia presentations offer students the opportunity to communicate something, learn and practice skills, gather and present information, and solve problems. As long as multimedia presentations include relevant content, they can be effective instructional tools in the classroom.

Multimedia Presentation Tips

✦ Help students make connections in more than one area. Have them do the following:

- choose a question, experiment, topic, etc., that relates to the real world.
- use their identities, everyday lives, backgrounds, and cultures to think of ideas for presentations.
- consider how the topic applies to their hobbies, sports, food, etc.
- draw on information learned from field trips or other class experiences.
- use newspaper and magazine articles to explore significant issues.
- think about how they can improve or change the real world by addressing real issues that affect their lives.

✦ Develop authentic interactions for research by having students do the following:

- conduct primary research.
- conduct their own interviews. (Encourage students to use e-mail to contact subject matter experts.)
- use photographs in their multimedia presentations.
- include relevant music in their multimedia presentations.

✦ Encourage students to present to real people. Have them do the following:

- Post comments on an actual teacher-approved blog.
- As a class, create a classroom blog. Respond to teacher-posted topics and student responses.
- In small groups, create websites that focus on classroom topics. (*Note:* Each group should focus on a different classroom topic.) Consider adding pictures and other graphics. Once finished, share each website with the class.
- In small groups, create videos that focus on classroom topics. (*Note:* Each group should focus on a different classroom topic.) Consider incorporating music and/or interviews. Once finished, share each video with the class.
- Make videos about their families and cultures. Share them with the class.
- Design webpages about a person they're studying in class. Share their webpages with parents or students in another class.

Making Connections *(cont.)*

Across the Content Areas	
Reading	Have students compare texts to their own experiences by asking questions, such as "What does this remind you of?" and "What does the text help you understand better?" Provide sentence frames (pg. 40) for students to make connections, such as "We read a(n) story (article) last week about _____," and "I think this story (article) might be about _____." Have students write journal entries to reflect on what they read.
Writing	Focus on the content of students' writing rather than exact grammatical correctness to encourage students' natural abilities to make connections to their own experiences. Illustrations help students make connections between new concepts and vocabulary and their background knowledge about a topic. Have students use ink to place their fingerprints on index cards. Encourage them to write their thoughts on the cards whenever they make personal connections to a specific aspect of the text.
Social Studies	Help students to identify keywords and make connections between these concepts and their cultures. Have students use graphic organizers (pg. 32) and brainstorming techniques (pg. 27) to make connections and understand social studies passages. Have students use K-W-L charts (pg. 35) to help identify what they already know about a social studies topic. Have students share personal experiences that remind them of the group of people being discussed.
Science	Help students recall other articles or passages they have read about the same science topic. Draw upon students' background knowledge and present science concepts within a multicultural framework. Use school or online resources to create a bilingual vocabulary list for a science unit of study in students' native languages.

Student Literacy Connections *(cont.)*
Strategies for Students *(cont.)*

Making Inferences

Students come to school with a variety of background experiences and language skills. Inference skills help students make accurate predictions about what they read, understand cause-and-effect relationships, and summarize information. Students use the context of what they read combined with what they already know to create meaning. Context clues, such as explanations or details, can help students solve problems, make decisions, or answer questions. Students use inference skills when they think beyond the text to understand what they read. This allows students to explore new meanings and make personal connections.

Tips for Teaching the Strategy

✦ Help students understand the inference process; they make inferences from what the text suggests but doesn't actually say.

✦ Define inference by writing a simple equation for class display

> **Inference**
>
> new information + prior knowledge
>
> = a reading discovery or
> an answer to a question

✦ Explain that the questions we ask ourselves when we read are natural inference questions. These include the following examples:

- What caused _____?

- Why?

- What do I already know about _____?

- What do I need to know about this topic?

- What do the illustrations (drawings, photographs, charts, tables) tell me about the topic?

- How does one thing I read relate to something else I read?

- Which information will help me answer a question or solve a problem?

- How has something I have read changed the way I feel about something?

✦ Explain that to make inferences means to draw conclusions about what a text means.

✦ Have students mark text (pg. 36) to identify clues that help readers make inferences.

✦ Tell students that when they make inferences, they use other skills, too, such as making predictions (pp. 62–63), using background knowledge (pg. 51), observing, and incorporating ideas.

Student Literacy Connections *(cont.)*
Strategies for Students *(cont.)*

Making Inferences *(cont.)*

Across the Content Areas	
Reading	Provide inference questions, such as the following, to help students develop their skills: "What do I already know about _____ (this character; this type of person)?" "Why did this person act in this way?" and "What do I already know about the event(s) described in the story?" Encourage students to connect details from different places in the text to understand the story as a whole. Have students use a reading or listening guide (pg. 39). Read poetry and discuss images and feelings from the reading.
Writing	Have students rehearse inference-related questions or statements from a reading assignment before writing sentences or a paragraph. Help students draw conclusions by asking them to think about something they saw in their neighborhoods or at school. Have them create graphic organizers by drawing a box in the center of their papers and then drawing several boxes around it. Students will draw arrows from the outer boxes pointing directly to the central box. In the outer boxes, they should write evidence that supports the conclusion they write in the center box. To *infer* means "to hint or suggest." Have students give partners hints about a story and then have the partners guess the story.
Social Studies	Show students an object related to a specific social studies event or group of people. Ask students the following questions: "What event does this object represent?" "What do I observe about this object?" "What does it tell me about this event, these people, or this place?" "How does this event still affect us today?" and "In what way(s) has the reading made me a better person?" Have students look at photographs to understand the past. Ask them to tell what they observe in the pictures. Have students compare what they read to their own experiences to draw conclusions about why people acted a certain way. Tell students to use what they have inferred, along with information from the text, to answer questions or solve a problem.
Science	Have students discuss examples in the science text to understand the main concept. Provide inference questions, such as the following, for students to guide their thinking when they conduct experiments: "What happened?" "Why did it happen?" and "What evidence supports my conclusion?" Students may list the steps or sequence of events they observed to help them form a conclusion. Have students use inference skills to ask questions (pg. 50), make predictions (pp. 62–63), form a hypothesis, and then use facts and evidence to draw conclusions when a direct observation can't be made (e.g., understanding what's inside Earth).

Student Literacy Connections *(cont.)*
Strategies for Students *(cont.)*

Making Predictions

Making predictions while they read helps students set a purpose for reading. Students use clues, such as the title, pictures, headings, and other text features to think about what they will read about in a story or article. Effective readers pause at different points in the selection and ask themselves if what they have read thus far confirms their predictions. Students' predictions may change as they read. When reading nonfiction text, have students think about what they already know to predict what new information they might learn as they read.

Tips for Teaching the Strategy

✦ Write the steps of the strategy in order, and explain to students how to do the following:

• predict (what you think will happen in a story or what you think you will learn)

• confirm (check to see if your predictions were correct)

• self-correct (make new predictions based on what you read)

✦ Help students observe text structure and format.

✦ Point out nonfiction text features, such as the title, table of contents, chapter headings, maps, and diagrams to help students think about what they might learn as they read.

✦ Remind students to use what they already know (background knowledge) to help them make predictions.

✦ Remind students to think about personal experiences when making predictions.

✦ Have students think about similar texts they have already read.

✦ Help students think about what they already know from the author using the following sentence frames:

• The author wrote this because _____.

• The author wants readers to know _____.

• I think (this information) will come next because _____.

✦ Have students identify (highlight) keywords, phrases, or text features that help them determine if their predictions are accurate. Encourage students to revise or make new predictions as needed.

✦ Use think-aloud techniques (pg. 43).

✦ Give an example to illustrate making predictions, such as this: "When you make predictions about what you read, it is like a weatherman forecasting the weather. He uses clues and what he knows to predict what might happen next."

✦ Motivate students to ask questions (pg. 50) that will help them make predictions. Model how to restate the questions as predictions.

Making Predictions *(cont.)*

	Across the Content Areas
Reading	Have students list the characteristics of an author (if students are familiar with more than one work by this author), text structure, or genre. Encourage students to focus on a character or main event and include details beyond basic predictions (e.g., "I think this story will be about . . . "). Have students think about the possibilities for a text. List one or two events in the story and then have students map out what might happen next. Have students place sticky notes next to the parts of the story in which they discover whether or not their predictions are correct. Do a think-aloud (pg. 43) to model how to make predictions for nonfiction text. Write six or seven words from the text on the board. Invite students to guess what the text will be about. (Don't give away the topic too easily.)
Writing	Have students write double-entry journals (pg. 30) to record their predictions and evidence from the text. Have students use graphic organizers (pg. 32) to help them make predictions as they read classmates' writing. Use a Directed Listening-Thinking Activity (pg. 29).
Social Studies	Discuss and identify key features of a social studies passage (such as headings or illustrations) to create an "I Notice" chart with the class. Help students identify patterns of behavior by asking questions, such as "How do you _____ each _____?" Create a simple bar or line graph to record predictions and actual evidence based on personal research. Create a game for students to guess what will happen next.
Science	Have students mark text (pg. 36) to list and number predictions and to relate their predictions to specific parts of the science text. Ask questions after reading and discuss responses to determine how well the prediction strategies worked. Explain that forming a hypothesis is like making a prediction. Use sentence frames (pg. 40) to scaffold student responses for experiments, such as "What will happen if we _____ to _____ ?" and "How does _____ work?" Use sentence frames to help students write sample hypotheses. Have students follow a reading or listening guide (pg. 39) while reading a science text.

Student Literacy Connections (cont.)
Strategies for Students (cont.)

Paraphrasing

One way to help students construct meaning is to paraphrase a text or concept. ELLs benefit from having key phrases or ideas stated in many different ways. Teachers can say or write concepts using different words or restate the definitions of new words.

Tips for Teaching the Strategy

✦ Paraphrase to repeat concepts.

✦ Help students identify the main idea.

✦ Have students mark text (pg. 36) to help them learn to paraphrase.

✦ Students may use synonyms or antonyms to restate something in other words.

✦ Have students include details and examples to describe a concept when they paraphrase.

✦ Ask students to paraphrase orally or in writing.

✦ If students seem uncomfortable paraphrasing orally, have them write paraphrases in their own words first. Some ELLs become more comfortable with written language first. Ask students to write about how they would explain something they heard or read to someone else.

Across the Content Areas	
Reading	Practice with a read-aloud experience (pg. 38). After students have heard the story or article, have them paraphrase to partners or buddies from another class, if possible.
Writing	Provide sentence frames (pg. 40), and ask students to rewrite the sentences. Provide an outline of the text for students to use when writing or saying their own paraphrases.
Social Studies	Have students write one or more keywords or phrases after reading a social studies passage and then trade papers with partners and write keywords or phrases based on their partners' paraphrases. Have students practice paraphrasing questions and answers from an existing worksheet activity.
Science	Have students rewrite or repeat oral or written directions in their own words. Have students practice asking partners direct questions about a science text. Partners will paraphrase with statements or questions to express their understanding (or lack thereof). The first student clarifies with a restatement, and the second student confirms his or her new understanding.

Summarizing

A summary restates the main points in a few sentences. It gives the general idea of a reading selection in a shorter form. When students summarize what they read, they use the skill of paraphrasing, or stating something in their own words. Learning to summarize helps students communicate to others what they read and learn.

Tips for Teaching the Strategy

✦ Help students determine important ideas in the text.

✦ Have students identify an essential question to understand what they read.

✦ Work together as a class to focus on key ideas and identify topic sentences in paragraphs and sections.

✦ Give students opportunities to practice finding the main idea (pg. 54).

✦ Ask students what they will do once they highlight (marking text, pg. 36) phrases or sentences. How will their markings help them to summarize what they have read?

✦ Use a timeline or chart to model (pg. 37) and think aloud (pg. 43) how to write a summary.

Across the Content Areas	
Reading	Have students use notes after reading to retell a story. Have students tell their versions of the story with partners and then record their partners' stories or words in order. Have students read texts, turn them over, and then write summaries.
Writing	Allow low-proficiency ELLs to use paper that has a blank space on top with lines on the bottom half of the page to draw and label pictures to summarize what they read and then write a summary. Have students use brainstorming techniques (pg. 27) to write summaries.
Social Studies	Have students participate in "buzz groups" in which they work in small groups to create summaries of a social studies selection and then present their summaries to the class. Have students listen to a social studies-related read-aloud (pg. 38) or video clip and write down the keywords and main points. Then have them give oral or written summaries.
Science	Have students read a science passage and then determine the important parts of the passage using the following steps: **1.** Ask questions (pg. 50). **2.** Evaluate what you read. **3.** Draw conclusions about the text. **4.** Determine what the text means. **5.** Recall what you read. Have students use sticky notes to notate the main idea and details (pg. 54).

Student Literacy Connections (cont.)
Strategies for Students (cont.)

Understanding Nonfiction Text Structures

Nonfiction writing, often called expository text, informs or describes. This type of writing appears in many forms, including textbooks, encyclopedias, magazine and newspaper articles, websites, and interviews. Each nonfiction text has a specific organizational structure, as well as text features, such as titles, chapters, headings, graphics, captions, and different types of print. Textbooks and other print materials are classroom tools; teach students how to use these tools just as you would teach them how to use other equipment in the classroom.

Tips for Teaching the Strategy

✦ Help students to identify nonfiction text features.

✦ Describe how nonfiction text is structured. Use "Organizational Structures of Nonfiction Text" (pg. 67) as a reference.

✦ Deconstruct a text to help students understand its organizational structure.

✦ Use the "Sample Glossary" (pg. 68) to teach related vocabulary. Then review the "Text Features Questions" (pg. 68) as is, or rewrite the questions as sentence frames.

✦ Use the "Sample Textbook Page" (pg. 69) to introduce text features.

✦ Prepare a sample reading guide for students to use when they read nonfiction text. Use the "Sample Reading Guide" (pg. 70) as a reference.

✦ Model a think-aloud (pg. 43), showing how "good readers" get information from text.

✦ Teach signal words. Words such as *for example, in conclusion, most important, therefore,* and *such as* tell the reader to pay attention.

✦ Help students make inferences (pp. 60–61) from photographs and illustrations. Remind students that graphics may contain important information.

✦ Point out that some nonfiction texts do not contain nonfiction text features (e.g., biographies, books about historic events), but they are still nonfiction.

Across the Content Areas	
Reading	Enlarge a page of expository text. Place numbers by various textbook features, such as headings, captions, bold print, etc. Provide a word card for each item. Have students work with partners to match the word cards to the numbers.
Writing	Have students work with partners to make "mock book" layouts.
Social Studies	Cover a picture or other graphic on a social studies textbook page, and have students create something to illustrate the page based on the information they read.
Science	Have students copy a diagram from a science textbook page and write their own captions for their drawings.

Understanding Nonfiction Text Structures *(cont.)*

Organizational Structures of Nonfiction Text	
Cause and Effect	Explains why something happens *Teaching Tip:* Provide a physical demonstration, such as sharpening a pencil.
Chronological Order	Presents events in the order in which they happened *Teaching Tip:* Describe a typical school day, emphasizing the order of subjects, recess, lunch, etc.
Classification	Describes common attributes of things *Teaching Tip:* Discuss the components of the food pyramid/plate.
Compare and Contrast	Describes how things are alike and/or different *Teaching Tip:* Use a Venn diagram or matrix to compare and contrast two stories or reading passages.
Descriptive	Describes specific characteristics of a subject *Teaching Tip:* Post a work of art, such as Van Gogh's *Starry Night* or M.C. Escher's *Waterfall*, and describe away!
Order of Importance	Arranges information in order, from least important to most important or from most important to least important *Teaching Tip:* Discuss a newspaper's layout—how articles are organized from most important (top of the page or front section) to least important (bottom of the page or subsequent pages).
Persuasive	Tries to get readers to agree with a particular idea or viewpoint *Teaching Tip:* Discuss an advertisement, as well as its effects.
Problem and Solution	Asks questions about how to change a difficult situation, and suggests ways to solve the problem *Teaching Tip:* Ask students for a sample problem. Then offer a solution.
Process	Describes how something happens *Teaching Tip:* Describe how to cook something, such as a grilled cheese sandwich.
Spatial Order	Describes things in physical relation to other things; describes a place *Teaching Tip:* Direct students to an area of the classroom that contains many objects. Describe their placement.

Student Literacy Connections (cont.)
Strategies for Students (cont.)

Understanding Nonfiction Text Structures: Sample Glossary and Text Features Questions

Photocopy and have students fold this page so the questions are hidden from view. Use the glossary to introduce and explain nonfiction text features and related vocabulary. Then have students unfold the page and review the features using the sample questions.

Glossary

bold print: letters or words that have heavy black lines

bullet: a small dot (or other symbol) used for emphasis at the beginning of a line of text

caption: a short title or description printed below a picture or drawing

chart: a drawing that shows information in the form of a table or graph

diagram: a drawing that explains something

glossary: one or more pages that give the meaning of certain words or phrases used in a book

graph: a diagram that shows the relationship between numbers or amounts

graphics: images such as drawings, maps, or graphs

heading: words written at the top of a page or over a section of writing in a magazine or book

illustration: a picture, drawing, diagram, sketch, or an example

italics: a slanted form of print used to emphasize certain words

map: a detailed plan of an area

picture: an image of something, such as a painting, photograph, or drawing

sidebar: a short article printed alongside a major news story that is a related subject

subtitle: a second or less important title of a book that explains more about the title

table: a chart that lists facts and figures, usually in columns

title: the name given to a book or chapter to identify or describe it

---

Text Features Questions

1. Where do you find the heading?
2. What is the purpose of a title?
3. How is a title different from a subtitle?
4. What graphics might you find in a nonfiction text?
5. Why would a graphic be placed in the text?
6. What does the caption tell you about a graphic?
7. Why might an author use bold print or italics?
8. Where do you look if you want to know what a word means?

Student Literacy Connections *(cont.)*
Strategies for Students *(cont.)*

Understanding Nonfiction Text Structures: Sample Textbook Page

Photocopy and use this sample textbook page (reading level 5.5) to introduce and explain nonfiction text features. Alternatively, use this page as a guide to label a photocopied page from a classroom textbook to provide students with familiar text.

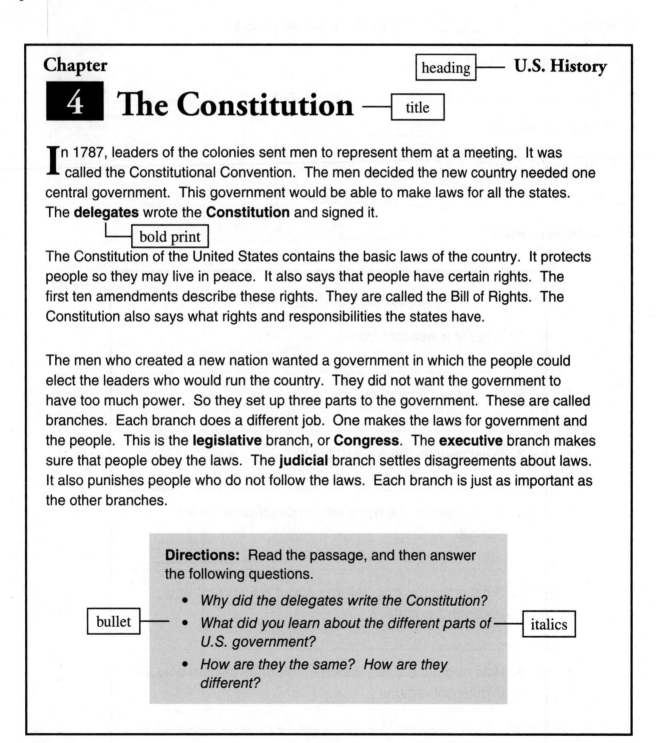

Chapter

heading — U.S. History

4 The Constitution — title

In 1787, leaders of the colonies sent men to represent them at a meeting. It was called the Constitutional Convention. The men decided the new country needed one central government. This government would be able to make laws for all the states. The **delegates** wrote the **Constitution** and signed it.

bold print

The Constitution of the United States contains the basic laws of the country. It protects people so they may live in peace. It also says that people have certain rights. The first ten amendments describe these rights. They are called the Bill of Rights. The Constitution also says what rights and responsibilities the states have.

The men who created a new nation wanted a government in which the people could elect the leaders who would run the country. They did not want the government to have too much power. So they set up three parts to the government. These are called branches. Each branch does a different job. One makes the laws for government and the people. This is the **legislative** branch, or **Congress**. The **executive** branch makes sure that people obey the laws. The **judicial** branch settles disagreements about laws. It also punishes people who do not follow the laws. Each branch is just as important as the other branches.

Directions: Read the passage, and then answer the following questions.

bullet

* *Why did the delegates write the Constitution?*
* *What did you learn about the different parts of* — italics *U.S. government?*
* *How are they the same? How are they different?*

Student Literacy Connections (cont.)
Strategies for Students (cont.)

Understanding Nonfiction Text Structures: Sample Reading Guide

Use this page as a reference when creating a reading guide for students. Each reading guide is specific to one textbook passage or reading selection and may have questions or statements that require students to supply one or more words. For more information on reading guides, see pg. 39.

◆ What is a _____? (use for vocabulary words)

◆ Name the (number) parts of _____.

◆ Why is _____ a good way to describe _____?

◆ What does it mean to say _____?

◆ What does the diagram on pg._____ show?

◆ What does _____ tell you about _____?

◆ What happens when _____?

Weather Reading Guide

1. What is a weather front?

   _____

2. Name the types of clouds.

   _____

3. What causes the wind to blow?

   _____

4. Why is *blizzard* a good way to describe a winter storm?

   _____

5. What does the map tell you about the current and upcoming weather?

   _____

6. How might the day's weather influence people who live in different regions?

   _____

Using Context Clues

Authors often use other words or phrases to help readers define new words. Students can use these clues to help them understand the meaning of what they read. Visual cues, such as pictures, charts, tables, and graphs can also provide clues to the text. Other context clues include punctuation, details, and examples. Context clues help students learn to read critically.

Tips for Teaching the Strategy

✦ Define the concept of context clues by telling students that they can use inference skills to figure out meaning from information given in the text.

✦ Teach only one type of context clue at a time. When appropriate, provide examples for each of the following:

- details and explanations
- definitions and restatements
- synonyms and antonyms
- examples
- compare and contrast

- cause and effect
- visual cues
- word order
- punctuation
- patterns

✦ Model with a think-aloud (pg. 43) to show how to use context clues.

✦ Ask students to make inferences (pp. 60–61) about characters' feelings and emotions based on clues in pictures and text.

✦ Show students how to use surrounding text to decode the meanings of new words by substituting words that might make sense in the sentence.

✦ Alert students to the order of words in a sentence, which can help them determine if the word they do not recognize is a noun, a verb, or another part of speech.

✦ Encourage students to use their background knowledge along with context clues.

Across the Content Areas	
Reading	Use brainstorming activities (pg. 27) to discuss as a class what students can do when they encounter words or phrases they don't understand while reading.
Writing	Invite students to play with language by changing a few words in a short passage to nonsense words. Be sure to include context clues, such as examples or synonyms. Have students guess what each word must mean based on the clues. Use this activity to lead into having students write summaries of the original passage.
Social Studies	Have students use context clues to make hypotheses about a social studies passage.
Science	Provide students with science passages that have new vocabulary words. Have students work in small groups to define the words or phrases, and have them explain how they used context clues.

Visualizing

Visualization helps students understand story structure. As they create pictures in their minds, students visualize what is happening in a story, which helps their comprehension. They use their senses as they imagine the scenes, allowing them to engage with the text. When students visualize, they also make connections with their prior knowledge. Visual literacy refers to the ability to interpret pictures and other visual images such as graphs or charts.

Tips for Teaching the Strategy

✦ Sketch words while modeling a think-aloud (pg. 43).

✦ Point to a picture and ask students simple questions, such as the following, to help them match what they see with what they imagine: "Do you see _____?" and "What does it make you think of?"

✦ Have students close their eyes and form mental pictures as you read. Start with a short selection with vivid descriptions.

✦ Read a passage with concrete objects. Invite students to visualize the shapes, colors, and spatial relationships of the objects. If there is any movement in the passage, have students describe that, as well.

✦ Read poetry to give students exposure to strong imagery.

✦ Create diagrams to help students visualize a process.

✦ Check student drawings to monitor comprehension.

Across the Content Areas	
Reading	Have students listen to a read-aloud (pg. 38). Ask them to draw pictures to show what they heard. Then have students describe and explain their drawings to partners. Use visualization techniques with readers' theater or other scripts (pg. 42). Have students draw scenes after hearing them.
Writing	Have students describe mental images or physical objects using a given number of adjectives. Have students write sentences, then read their sentences aloud to partners. The partners will describe the mental images they have from listening to the sentences that were read aloud.
Social Studies	Provide a reading guide (pg. 39) to help students create mental pictures as they read their social studies text. Use visualization techniques to summarize longer passages.
Science	Help students interpret science charts, graphs, tables, and photographs. Use diagrams and other graphic representations to help students learn science concepts and vocabulary at the same time.

Across the Curriculum
Language Objectives

Language objectives should incorporate the standards students will meet as they learn to use English in academic settings. Include language objectives as part of lessons to help students learn the words and grammatical structures they will need to access and make meaning out of academic content.

- ✦ Know what you want students to learn.

- ✦ Incorporate language objectives as part of content-area lesson plans.

- ✦ Refer to ELL standards to write language objectives.

- ✦ Be as specific as possible.

- ✦ Relate objectives to the lesson and preview objectives with students.

- ✦ Language objectives include discipline-specific language, academic language, and how language is used in the classroom.

- ✦ Consider the four language domains when writing language objectives: listening, speaking, reading, and writing.

- ✦ Help students meet language objectives by checking for understanding, summarizing, and defining terms and concepts as you teach.

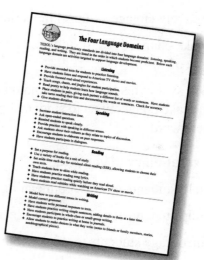

- ✦ Explain that language skills help students to accomplish the following:

  - • explain
  - • defend
  - • describe
  - • discuss
  - • identify
  - • summarize
  - • compare and contrast

Examples of Language Objectives

- ✦ Students will write in complete sentences using capital letters and ending punctuation marks.

- ✦ Students will verbally describe what happens when someone takes a breath of air.

- ✦ Students will read their assigned passage and give verbal summaries in groups.

Across the Curriculum *(cont.)*
Extending Vocabulary

Much of the academic vocabulary students need to learn applies to multiple content areas. Make instruction more comprehensible by using the provided strategies and activities below to help students extend their vocabulary in meaningful ways.

Create an awareness of words.

+ Create a word-rich environment.

+ Introduce new words with flash cards.

+ Ask students what they notice about a word.

+ Model a think-aloud (pg. 43), showing how to use rhyming strategies.

+ Have students create a symbol or sketch to help them remember what a word means.

+ Connect vocabulary to prior knowledge.

+ Give students a purpose for learning new words.

+ Actively engage students in learning new vocabulary.

+ Make connections to students' cultures and personal experiences (pp. 57–59).

+ Use synonyms, antonyms, and other words students already know to make connections to students' prior knowledge and teach new words.

Teach vocabulary in context.

+ Help students infer word meanings from context.

+ Help students understand the meaning of a word as it is used in context or in a question.

+ Encourage students to think about how to use the word.

+ Apply new vocabulary in a familiar context.

+ Give examples of how new words are used correctly and incorrectly in sentences.

+ Draw students' attention to any visual clues provided in the context.

+ Have students complete sentence frames (pg. 40).

+ Create ways for students to use new words in a variety of contexts.

+ Help students make connections if words relate to one another, for example, words that express emotions.

+ Use focused questions to assess students' understanding of new words used in context.

Give students direct instruction.

✦ Provide meaningful definitions for new words.

✦ Teach word study skills to help students learn word parts (roots, prefixes, suffixes), families, and cognates, if applicable.

✦ Preteach vocabulary and concepts. Use materials in ELLs' native languages or at their levels of English proficiency, if possible.

✦ Use gestures or hand motions to preteach vocabulary. Have students mimic the gestures.

✦ Use visual aids to explain terms (pg. 44).

✦ Use Internet resources to find pictures to go with vocabulary terms.

✦ Model ways to understand new words: Look for punctuation and other context clues, use a glossary, or ask for help (pg. 37).

✦ Explain compound words.

✦ Preteach common command verbs, such as *describe* and *explain*, so students understand what is being asked of them.

✦ Preteach, demonstrate, and explain idioms and special phrases. Compare the literal meaning and the intended meaning.

✦ Check for understanding of vocabulary or content-area words.

✦ Teach students about homophones and homographs.

✦ Teach transition words and sequence words, such as the following:

• after(wards)	• however	• since
• also	• if	• so
• although	• in addition	• soon
• and	• in other words	• then
• at first	• last(ly)	• therefore
• at last	• later	• third
• because	• more(over)	• though
• before	• next	• until
• but	• now	• while
• finally	• or	• yet
• first	• second	
• for	• similarly	

Across the Curriculum *(cont.)*
Extending Vocabulary *(cont.)*

Incorporate vocabulary instruction throughout the day.

✦ Use simple, everyday language to teach students the meanings of new words.

✦ Draw or illustrate new words.

✦ Help students learn oral and written versions of words at the same time.

✦ Have students write and pronounce new words correctly as a group.

✦ Have students use new vocabulary in speaking practice in the classroom.

✦ Apply learned vocabulary to new instructional topics.

✦ Expose students to new words in different formats and contexts.

✦ Encourage students to ask questions about words.

✦ Expand on students' questions to define specific terms.

✦ Have classmates explain new terms to each other.

✦ Encourage students to share new, appropriate words they have learned outside of class, at home, and in the community.

✦ Create word webs to expand vocabulary. Warm up with a think-pair-share activity (pg. 43) to get students thinking about the topic.

✦ Create daily word charts to help students sort words by patterns and meaning.

✦ Have students classify and sort words by spelling patterns.

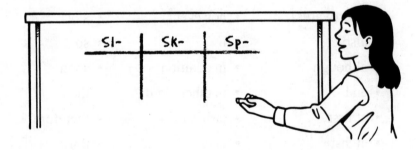

Activities to Extend Vocabulary

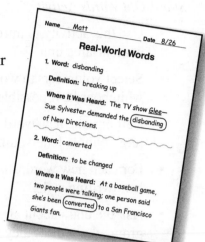

✦ Give students credit for finding vocabulary word(s) used in real-world situations. Have students write down the words, their definitions, and where they were heard.

✦ Ask students to generate examples and non-examples of vocabulary words used in context.

✦ Have students use new words they have learned when they compose original stories, articles, or blog posts.

✦ Have students work together to create a word mural. Students will incorporate visual cues and the ways the words might be used, along with definitions.

✦ Read each vocabulary word and its definition one word at a time. Have students write sentences about themselves using each word.

✦ Invite students to rewrite the lyrics to a current popular song. If possible, use culturally universal tunes. They should include as many vocabulary words as possible.

✦ Have students create their own graphic organizers that define new words. Remind students to keep their organizers handy for reference when they read.

✦ Invite students to create riddles, giving clues for other classmates to guess the correct vocabulary words.

✦ Demonstrate highlighting new vocabulary in one color. Highlight repetitions (repeated uses of the word, synonyms, explanations, or definitions in context) in another color.

✦ Provide a context and ask the class which vocabulary word best applies in the new context. Invite students to submit their own sentences for class discussion.

✦ Have students sort words by meaning or other criteria.

✦ Create a rebus for students.

✦ Have students create their own rebuses.

✦ *Class Word Project*

  • Have students collect words for a class glossary or dictionary. Ask students to choose the words they want to learn.

  • Have students talk with each other about why they chose those words for the class word project.

  • Make sure students understand the meanings of the new words and are given opportunities to use the words in classroom conversations and writing.

  • Encourage students to make personal connections when they encounter these words in their reading.

✦ *Stand-Out Words Activity*

- Use this activity to introduce new vocabulary at the beginning of a word study or content-area unit.

- Select volunteers to work at the board. Have the rest of the class follow along on individual whiteboards, if possible.

- Call out one new word at a time. Students will write each word as creatively as possible (e.g., bubble letters, different colors).

- For each new word, students will move to a new space on the board and change their handwriting style.

- Ask the class about any usual combinations of words represented; discuss how students grouped words as they moved from one space to another on the board and why the words might be grouped in that way.

- Have students write a few sentences about how to use the new words or to reflect on the activity in general.

- Ask a few students to read their sentences aloud.

✦ *Targeting Words Activity*

- Select three or four words from a reading selection to target for vocabulary instruction. Choose words that students will encounter in other settings.

- Help students make associations between the target words and other words they know. Use synonyms, antonyms, and other words with which the target words are commonly associated.

- Have students define the words in their own words. Model first and then practice as a whole class before having students work on their own.

- Remind them to compare their definitions with the dictionary definitions.

- Reinforce the correct meanings of the words as necessary.

- Have students find examples of the target words in the reading passage.

- Students may write their own sentences with the words, if desired.

Across the Curriculum *(cont.)*
Making Sense Out of Textbooks

Most textbooks are written in academic language. Passages have complex sentence structures and specific terms ELLs may not understand. Textbooks also assume that readers have background knowledge in specific areas. Help ELLs navigate textbooks using the following suggestions.

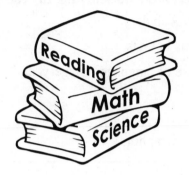

- ✦ Preview text features.
- ✦ Have students make predictions (pp. 62–63) about the text.
- ✦ Adapt textbook reading.
- ✦ Modify language as needed.
- ✦ Use alternate formats as necessary.
- ✦ Use simple descriptions.
- ✦ Teach students how to find keywords.
- ✦ Give concrete examples.
- ✦ Group items into categories for students to learn.
- ✦ Divide long sections of text into smaller passages.
- ✦ Explain any cultural assumptions the text makes.
- ✦ Discuss the questions in the book as a class, and then have students read the text. Review with questions again, if desired.
- ✦ Clarify text (pg. 52).
- ✦ Write keywords from the textbook selection on the board for reference as students read.
- ✦ Help students comprehend the meaning.
- ✦ Explain unfamiliar words, multiple-meaning words, signal words, or transition words.
- ✦ Use visual aids, including diagrams (pg. 44).
- ✦ Use manipulatives, gestures, or drawings.
- ✦ Use rubrics.

Across the Curriculum *(cont.)*
Reading Activities

ELLs benefit from reading methods and strategies used with native English speakers. However, they need additional support in vocabulary development, fluency, and motivation. Some aspects of language that native English speakers learn indirectly affect the ease with which ELLs learn to read in English. Consider the factors below when planning lessons, and use the provided tips and activities to increase comprehension.

Factors that affect students learning to read English include the following:

- ◆ unfamiliar vocabulary
- ◆ use of idioms in texts
- ◆ figurative use of language, imagery, and symbolism
- ◆ literary terms
- ◆ similes and metaphors

- ◆ homophones and homographs
- ◆ "exceptions to the rules" in grammar
- ◆ word order
- ◆ sentence structure

General Tips

- ◆ Modify instruction using visual, kinesthetic, or concrete references so that students can touch, feel, or see.
- ◆ Have students read a series of texts with the same characters, plotline, and conflict.
- ◆ Use a variety of print materials, such as the following, to give students plenty of practice:
    - instructions
    - handouts
    - newspapers
    - magazines
    - song lyrics
    - letters
    - short stories
    - recipes
- ◆ Select reading materials of interest to students, such as these:
    - comic books
    - graphic novels
    - stories
    - poems
    - nonfiction texts
    - multicultural literature

Teach students how to do the following:

- ✦ preview reading material.
- ✦ locate topic sentences.
- ✦ find supporting details.
- ✦ identify introductions and conclusions.
- ✦ predict outcomes.
- ✦ understand story themes and endings.
- ✦ skim to find facts.

Pre-Reading Activities

- ✦ Preview and discuss unfamiliar vocabulary ELLs might not easily understand.
- ✦ Preview text for words with multiple meanings, metaphors, or idioms.
- ✦ Preview text length and sentence structure to help students with their reading.
- ✦ Preview text features.
- ✦ Build text-specific knowledge by describing characters, ideas, or concepts.
- ✦ Use pre-questioning and predictions to set the direction and purpose for reading.
- ✦ Draw on students' background knowledge.
- ✦ Relate reading to students' lives.
- ✦ Consider how closely students need to read the text to accomplish the purpose.
- ✦ Have students read for meaning. Tell them they don't have to know every word to understand a passage.

Post-Reading Activities

- ✦ Reteach difficult words and concepts.
- ✦ Use oral-reading activities to communicate understanding and comprehension of text that students read silently.
- ✦ Use a story chart to have students identify the themes in a story. Ask students what the main character was trying to do.
- ✦ Read a selection more than once, and discuss a different aspect of the text each time.
- ✦ Discuss sequence to understand when and why things happen in a story.
- ✦ Have students talk about and summarize the text in small groups or as a class.

Across the Curriculum *(cont.)*
Writing Activities

Writing requires the ability to process language to communicate ideas. Writing helps students remember what they thought about a text; it enables them to respond to what they read.

Students' cultural backgrounds and previous educational experiences may influence how they approach the task of writing. In some cultures, students submit their "rough drafts" as "final copies" for the teacher to correct. These students will not be familiar with our writing process, in which students revise their rough drafts and write final copies before turning in the assignment. In other cultures, students adopt a storytelling style, in which much background information is introduced before getting to the main point. These students will need direct instruction in the concept of topic sentences and organizing writing for different purposes.

General Tips

✦ Use writing as a learning tool to promote language development.

✦ Scaffold students as they learn to write in English.

✦ Match writing activities to ELL development needs.

✦ Provide authentic purposes for writing.

✦ Guide students through the process of writing down what they say. This helps them make connections between oral and written language.

✦ Use props to get students started with the theme or topic for writing.

✦ Use photographs, posters, or other graphics and visual aids for writing.

✦ Introduce games to help students develop word knowledge and spelling skills.

✦ Suggest authentic publishing options for student writing.

✦ Allow students to make choices in what they write (e.g., notes to friends or parents, stories).

✦ Have students look at examples that begin with a topic idea and have an ending that lets the reader know the writer is finished.

Pre- and Post-Reading Activities

✦ Introduce a variety of types of writing. Have students experiment with the following:

- wordless picture books to encourage students to write and develop their own story lines.

- journal writing for personal expression.

- poetry writing to learn expressive language.

- descriptive writing to include a main idea and details.

- descriptive writing about a historic event or scientific phenomenon.

- comparative writing to compare and contrast concepts, procedures, or stories.

✦ Model the writing process and talk with students about what you are writing. Show examples, if desired.

✦ Use brainstorming activities (pg. 27) to generate a list of ideas for writing. Use one or more of these ideas as a starting point for a writing activity.

✦ Allow students to write their first drafts in their native languages then translate using one of the translation websites listed on pg. 110.

✦ Have students copy sentences or paragraphs to learn language structure.

✦ Allow students to dictate their ideas in small groups first.

✦ Offer cloze activities (pg. 28) for students to express their ideas using learned vocabulary or a word bank.

✦ Conduct a shared writing activity after students have participated in a class experience. Invite students to say sentences about the experience and write them exactly as stated on the board. When the story is complete, discuss any changes needed.

✦ Have students write on their own and allow them to refer to a text and retell it in their own words.

✦ Have students write stories or articles modeled on a class reading experience. For example, if students have recently read a biography, have them use a graphic organizer, such as an attribute web, to identify main ideas and details in the reading selection. Then have them use a similar graphic organizer to research, plan, and write short biography pieces on their own about the same person or someone different.

✦ Have students write in response to a prompt.

✦ Teach students how to participate in free-writing activities:

- Write for a set amount of time.

- Do not stop writing.

- Keep writing, even if you don't know what to write.

✦ Have students re-read their journals and use their writing as a prompt or starting point for additional writing activities.

Across the Curriculum *(cont.)*
Social Studies Activities

Social studies, by definition, relates to one or more specific cultures. ELLs may not have the cultural background knowledge necessary to understand social studies texts. Some concepts, such as privacy, personal property, and democracy vary from culture to culture, and ELLs may need direct instruction.

General Tips

✦ Apply academic standards to textbooks and other social studies reading materials and make connections using keywords and concepts.

✦ Break text into smaller parts with visual diagrams.

✦ Teach students how to take notes.

✦ Have students use visualization techniques (pg. 72) as they read.

✦ Help ELLs make connections to their own lives and experiences so they can remember what they've learned.

✦ Encourage ELLs to talk with family members in their native languages about what they are learning in social studies.

✦ Provide a safe environment in which students can express their opinions.

✦ Help students understand and use primary and secondary sources.

Pre-Reading Activities

✦ Introduce students to unfamiliar historical terms and vocabulary.

✦ Preteach, demonstrate, and explain idioms and phrases.

✦ Introduce sentence structures, including complex sentences, passive voice, and use of pronouns.

✦ Refer to "Understanding Nonfiction Text Structures" (pp. 66–70) to preview and introduce text features before students read.

✦ Provide background knowledge about U.S. history, geography, and current events.

✦ ELLs may not be familiar with various forms of government. As a class, compare simple government principles across cultures.

✦ Help students understand movement within the structure of a society (e.g., moving from a rural area to an urban area).

Across the Curriculum *(cont.)*
Social Studies Activities *(cont.)*

Pre-Reading Activities *(cont.)*

✦ Provide plenty of practice with map skills, as ELLs may be unfamiliar with maps.

✦ Have students use double-entry journals (pg. 30) to make predictions, conduct simple social experiments, and record actual results.

✦ Use guided reading strategies (pg. 33) to help ELLs comprehend content.

Post-Reading Activities

✦ Paraphrase sections of text during class discussions.

✦ Clarify meaning by replacing pronouns with nouns to help students understand what they read.

✦ Have native English speakers work with ELL partners to rephrase passive voice sentences. ("A law was passed by Congress" becomes "Congress passed a law.")

✦ Have students work in groups to review material.

✦ Ask ELLs to contribute alternate views that reflect conditions in other countries.

✦ Provide sentence frames (pg. 40), such as the following, to support students in reading and writing:

  • I already know _____ about _____ (topic).

  • This _____ (group of people) did _____ because _____.

  • After reading about _____ (group of people), I know that a typical day for them was _____.

✦ Invite students to write reflective paragraphs.

✦ Have students participate in role-playing exercises.

✦ Use if-then sentences to teach cause and effect.

✦ Compare timelines with other ways of understanding periods in history, such as dynasties.

✦ Have students compare and contrast themselves and their lives with a topic of study (e.g., Rome).

✦ Have students participate in a survey and include themselves.

✦ Conduct social experiments in class, and have students develop data sheets.

✦ Students can discuss concepts with peers and connect to others with similar or differing viewpoints. Conduct a class debate with opposing viewpoints on issues.

✦ Have students participate in an interactive activity. One student takes a turn reading and then reacts with a question or comment. Other students may comment on the first student's remark and/or continue reading.

Across the Curriculum (cont.)

Science Activities

Science presents a challenge for many students. This subject introduces complex concepts and vocabulary words not used in everyday conversations. Even though hands-on learning can help ELLs, science experiments may contain detailed steps that are hard for students to understand.

General Tips

✦ Help students understand the "hands-on" approach.

✦ Introduce ELLs to science labs or equipment (e.g., magnifying glasses, microscopes, balances) and give expectations for classroom behavior.

✦ Introduce students to specific text structures used in science reading material.

✦ Rephrase difficult sentence structure and passive voice, if possible.

✦ Explain visuals in text. Create simplified visuals, if necessary.

✦ Clarify meaning with diagrams.

✦ Cover material more slowly.

✦ Break science passages into "chunks," or smaller sections.

✦ Introduce students to the scientific method.

　• Help students understand the concept of hypothesis.

　• Teach students how and why to form conclusions.

✦ Give directions for experiments and procedures in simplified steps.

✦ Help students with vocabulary. Some words have different meanings in science (e.g., *work, power*).

✦ Help students learn the language of science (words and concepts such as *observe, describe, compare, classify, evaluate, conclude, record,* etc.).

✦ Teach students how and why they will work in cooperative groups (pg. 28).

✦ Explain that science, math, and technology are interdependent. If students have background knowledge or experience in math (such as measurement skills) or technology (ability to use the Internet to view scientific graphs and other visual representations), this will help them understand what they read in a science textbook.

Pre- and Post-Reading Activities

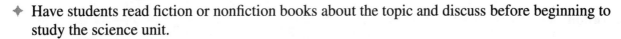

✦ As a class, discuss previous science experiences, including those outside of class (e.g., weather). Have students write and draw about their experiences related to the topic at hand.

✦ Relate one lesson to the next by using overviews and outlines that show students how the science curriculum fits together.

✦ Teach the parts of a science experiment, which include the following:

- overview/objectives
- materials
- preparation
- hypothesis
- procedure
- discussion
- record sheet
- conclusion

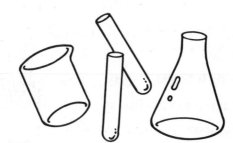

✦ Have students read fiction or nonfiction books about the topic and discuss before beginning to study the science unit.

✦ Provide hands-on activities (pg. 33) to introduce a unit.

✦ Prepare flash cards to help students learn words and the relationship between terms.

✦ Use games to teach new vocabulary words.

✦ Use closed-captioning on science videos to give students visual word clues to accompany new vocabulary they hear.

✦ Use visual aids (pg. 44) to help students understand a process or a conclusion.

✦ Have students explain the processes or concepts to each other. If necessary, students may use their native languages to explain complex concepts to each other first.

✦ Have students use double-entry journals (pg. 30) to record their predictions and actual results of experiments.

✦ Have students use Venn diagrams to compare two methods, processes, or outcomes.

✦ Display results using charts.

✦ Provide sentence frames (pg. 40), such as "If I did this experiment again, I would _____." (In other words, how would you change the experiment?)

✦ Have students work in small groups to discuss ideas, exchange information, and ask questions.

✦ If time and resources permit, prepare a list of websites for students to explore to help them become familiar with a science topic.

Across the Curriculum *(cont.)*

Sample Lesson: Using Text Features to Increase Reading Comprehension

Objective of the Reading Lesson

Give students an introduction to punctuation marks and other marks in a text selection. Students will write sentences, explain their responses, and discuss how such marks help readers understand text.

Materials

- ✦ arrow cutouts or icons
- ✦ cardstock (optional)
- ✦ sample text selection, one copy for class display
- ✦ sample charts or other diagrams for class display
- ✦ index cards, one or two per student
- ✦ drawing paper, one piece per student
- ✦ colored pencils for each student

Preparation

1. Cut two basic arrow shapes from cardstock for display on a whiteboard or chart, or have ready an arrow icon to display on an interactive whiteboard.

2. Prepare the following sentence frame for ELLs to complete by writing on a whiteboard, posting to a chart or wall display, or entering text into an interactive whiteboard.

    The text feature _____ helps me understand what I read by _____ .

Opening

1. Introduce a graphic representation. Write on the board or display on an interactive whiteboard the following:

> Text Features
> ↓
> Reading Comprehension

2. Ask students what this statement might mean.

3. Introduce sample charts and other diagrams and discuss how these visual aids can help readers understand text.

Directions

1. Display a sample text selection. As a class, point out and discuss punctuation marks. Explain that authors use punctuation marks and other markings, such as bold print, underlining, and italicized fonts, to cue readers to the meaning of the text.

2. Have students identify examples and tell how the markings make it easier to understand text.

3. Distribute one or two index cards per student. Have students identify one or more punctuation marks or other specific text features and write each one on a card. Have students write phrases or sentences to explain how each text feature helps them understand what they read.

4. Have students explain their responses to the class. Monitor the discussion and clarify as needed.

Closing

Invite students to turn their completed sentence frames into cartoon drawings to display in the classroom. Remind students to refer to the completed sentence frames or cartoon drawings as they read, so they'll remember to use text features to increase their reading comprehension.

ELL Tip

Ask volunteers to place their cards appropriately to complete the following sentence frame:

The text feature _____ helps me understand what I read by _____.

Across the Curriculum *(cont.)*
Sample Lesson: Finding Information

Objective of the Reading Lesson

Students will use what they have learned about nonfiction text structures to locate specific information in a text.

Materials

✦ prepared statements, facts, or hints of information

✦ one or more text selections, one copy per student

✦ poster board and appropriate markers

✦ patterned sentences at ELLs' reading levels (optional for small group work)

Preparation

1. Use different colors to highlight sample facts or bits of information in a sample nonfiction text to display in class.

2. Identify and write clues to read to students for each fact.

3. If using an overhead projector, have corresponding colored markers available for students. If using an interactive whiteboard, have colored arrows ready for students to drag and drop on the screen.

4. Prepare statements, facts, or hints of information that students will find in a text.

Opening

1. Display a sample page of nonfiction text using an overhead projector or interactive whiteboard.

2. Read one clue at a time for each fact. Have volunteers use colored markers to draw arrows or drag and drop arrows to identify the fact or information bit that matches each clue.

Directions

1. Model how to find a specific fact or piece of information. Write the fact, such as the following, on the board: "Wind and rain break large rocks into smaller pieces."

2. Provide a statement or hint about information students will look for in a text, such as "Find a clue that tells what weather does to rocks."

3. Focus their attention on locating information by asking questions, such as "What am I looking for?"

4. Tell students to look for clues in the text by doing the following:

   • looking for keywords, such as the weather words or rocks
   • skimming—checking headings, looking for keywords, and grouping words into phrases
   • looking at pictures or other graphics and illustrations

5. Remind students to use what they learned about noticing the differences between facts and opinions.

Directions *(cont.)*

6. As a class, discuss other ways students can locate information in a text (e.g., looking ahead, re-reading a passage, using a graphic organizer).

7. Distribute prepared statements and text selections. Have students read and locate specific information. Students should write down the sentence that contains the information. Have them write a page number, if appropriate.

8. Have students write the "answer," a fact, or another piece of information from the text selection for partners to find.

Closing

Have students create posters depicting what they did to find information in text. If possible, share the posters with another class.

ELL Tips

✦ Work with students in small groups, walking through sections of text and finding information.

✦ Have students write down the page number where they found the information for the class activity to check for accuracy.

✦ Provide patterned sentences at grade-level reading as part of the clues, which help students learn nonfiction text structure.

Across the Curriculum *(cont.)*
Sample Lesson: Asking Questions

Objective of the Reading, Science, or Social Studies Lesson

Through brainstorming activities and class discussion, students will learn how to ask
questions and practice doing so.

Materials

✦ whiteboard, chart paper, or overhead transparency
and appropriate markers

✦ *I Spy* or similar books with many pictures that
invite questioning

Opening

1. Brainstorm (pg. 27) how asking questions can help students
think and learn about new things. For example, questions . . .

   • give me a purpose for reading.

   • help me focus on what I read.

   • help me think.

   • help me review what I have already read.

2. As a class, create a graphic organizer (pg. 32) to help students remember key points of the
discussion.

3. Teach or review basic question words (*who, what, where, when, why, how*).

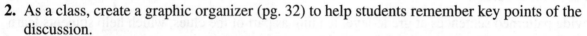

Directions

1. Discuss other ways to ask questions, such as the following:

   • Restate a statement as a question.

   • Ask about steps in a process.

   • Ask questions to solve a problem.

   • Use keywords, such as *describe*, *discover*, and *explain*.

2. Explain that when students ask questions, the answers might be explicitly stated or implied in
the text.

3. Introduce various types of questions, such as the following:

   • The answer is obvious in the text.

   • The question requires readers to read back through the text to find an answer that might be
   in one or more places in the text.

   • Students use their background knowledge about the topic and what they read from the text
   to answer the questions.

   • Questions are based entirely on the reader's background and experiences. These questions
   help students make connections to their own lives.

4. When students ask questions, it helps them determine how well they understand what they
are reading.

Directions *(cont.)*

5. Encourage students to ask questions that require them to put together information from different parts of the text.

6. Review how to answer questions using complete sentences.

7. Consider having students work together as a class to compile the lesson information about questions into a chart that students can refer to when reading content-area materials.

8. Have objects or books, such as *I Spy*, available. Invite students to ask questions about the objects and pictures.

9. Ask students to write down their questions to discuss later in class or with small groups.

Closing

1. Invite students to create a "quiz" for classmates. Students will write questions about a text selection or a topic of current study for partners to answer.

2. Remind students to phrase or write their answers as complete sentences.

ELL Tip

Help students practice asking or writing questions. Have students first make statements about the object. Then help them turn their statements into questions, such as the following:

> The pencil is orange.
>
> ↓
>
> What color is the pencil?

Across the Curriculum *(cont.)*
Sample Lesson: Making Inferences

> ### Objective of the Reading, Social Studies, or Science Lesson
> Given a review of inference, students will read a selection and use clues to answer questions about the meaning of what they read.

Materials

+ clue cards
+ sample story or nonfiction text, one copy per student
+ additional reading materials
+ sticky notes, two or three per student

Why is the stone special

Why is the mirror kept in a secret room?

Preparation

Prepare clue cards for a story to create a simple game in which students predict what they think will happen in a story. On each card, write one clue to help students infer meaning from the story or passage. In addition to the clue, write one or more questions that students can use the clue to answer.

Opening

1. Review with students how to make inferences (pp. 60–61).
2. Remind students that they can use context clues, such as explanations or details, to determine what the text means or use context clues to answer questions.
3. Tell students that they will use clues to find answers to questions about what they read when the answer may not be explicitly stated in the text.
4. Give each student a clue card and a copy of the related reading passage. Students will read their clues and the reading passage and then answer the questions on the cards.

Directions

1. Students will read a short story or nonfiction reading selection independently.
2. Then have students write clues for partners on sticky notes.
3. Have students use what they learned about asking questions to write questions for their partners.
4. Have students trade clues, questions, and reading selections with partners.
5. Partners will use the clues to figure out something about the story that the author does not state directly.

Closing

Invite students to create games using clues to infer meaning from a variety of reading materials or experiences. Encourage them to think of clues and questions that help them develop skills of inference.

ELL Tips

+ Have students read a passage together in small groups.
+ Have them verbalize their clues and questions before they write them down.
+ Allow students to work together to solve the clues and answer the questions.

Across the Curriculum (cont.)
Sample Lesson: My Past in Writing

Objective of the Writing Lesson
Students will write and ask interview questions to learn about classmates' writing experiences.

Materials

student journals, one per student

Opening

1. Review what students have learned about asking questions.

2. Discuss how they feel and what their preferences are when other people ask them questions (e.g., polite or respectful tone of voice, other person listens to their answers, the question is not rude or too personal).

3. Discuss asking and answering questions in the context of students' cultural backgrounds, including what is appropriate and acceptable in a culture, if applicable.

Directions

1. Think aloud (pg. 43) to introduce the topic of past writing experiences.

2. Have students think about their past writing experiences. Ask students to write reflective journal entries about the role writing has played in their personal or cultural backgrounds.

3. Refer back to the opening discussion and teach students how to ask questions in writing using the following steps:
   - Be brief and simple.
   - State the question in one sentence.
   - Use precise words to say what you want to say.
   - Phrase the question clearly.
   - Begin the question with a capital letter and end it with a question mark.

4. Once students have considered their own writing experiences, have them think of and write questions to ask classmates about past writing experiences.

5. Pair up students to conduct the interviews.

6. When answering interview questions, students may refer to their written journal entries as necessary.

Closing

Provide opportunities for students to share interview responses with the class. They may introduce their partners to the class, saying, "Katka is a writer. She has written an invitation to her birthday party."

ELL Tip

Accept different types of written communication as past writing experiences.

Across the Curriculum *(cont.)*

Sample Lesson: Comparing and Contrasting Cultures

Objective of the Writing Lesson

Students will compare their own cultures with classmates' cultures that are different from their own.

Materials

graphic organizers appropriate for comparing and contrasting (pg. 32), one copy per student and one copy for class display

Opening

1. Remind students that every culture is unique, interesting, and worth learning about.

2. Ask students to think about their own cultures. This includes thinking about traditions, customs, and values. Tell them to also reflect on the holidays, foods, and clothing embraced by their cultures.

3. Review what students have learned about using graphic organizers to compare and contrast.

4. Discuss asking and answering questions in the context of students' cultural backgrounds. Remind students to be respectful and open-minded concerning their classmates' backgrounds.

Directions

1. Think aloud (pg. 43) to introduce your own culture. Use a sample graphic organizer to document your cultural information.

2. Have students think about their cultures. Ask them to write noteworthy cultural information on one side of the organizer.

3. Pair up students so they can work with individuals who have had different cultural experiences.

4. Have students interview each other about their cultures, writing the information on the other side of the organizer.

5. Have students review the cultural information (theirs and their partners') and compare and contrast, using the center part of the organizer to write their responses.

Closing

Provide opportunities for students to share information about their cultures. Students can also share information about their partners' cultures.

ELL Tip

Have students write journal entries or free-writes on cultures they learned about from this lesson (and didn't know about before).

Across the Curriculum *(cont.)*
Sample Lesson: Taking a Test

Objective of the Lesson

Students will read a short passage and practice taking notes to answer sample test questions.

Materials

✦ "United States Regions" (reading level 5.4; 367 words) (pg. 100) or similar passage, one copy per student and one copy for class display

✦ various graphic organizers (pg. 32) for class display

✦ scrap paper, one piece per student

✦ sample test (pg. 101), one copy per student and one copy for class display

Opening

1. Display the sample test. Ask the following questions to engage students in a discussion about taking a test:

   • How does this test look the same as other tests you have seen? How does it look different?

   • What makes a test easy?

   • What is the hardest thing about taking a test?

   • What can you tell others to help them take a test?

2. Take note of differences in ELLs' background knowledge and expectations regarding tests.

Directions, Part I

1. Display the reading passage and distribute copies to the class. Read through the passage together, using a selected strategy from "Reading Activities" (pp. 80–81).

2. Give each student a piece of scrap paper. Tell students that they will use the scrap paper to take notes instead of marking on the reading passage. Explain that they often will not be able to write on a test.

3. Ask students to identify keywords, main ideas, and details. Have students write related keywords and phrases on their pieces of scrap paper.

4. Display samples of graphic organizers. Tell the class that another way to remember what they read is to take notes on a graphic organizer. Ask students to suggest a graphic organizer that would be effective for the sample reading passage.

5. Have volunteers share their notes about the main idea(s) in the passage (e.g., U.S. regions, climate, landforms).

6. Work together as a class to complete a graphic organizer. Ask students how this information might help them answer questions on a test. (Sample answer: They can look for keywords or phrases in the answer choices to help them find the correct answers.)

7. Have students read the sample passage again silently or with partners.

Directions, Part II

1. Distribute copies of the sample test.

2. Preview the test, reviewing how to read directions and mark answer choices clearly. Remind students to read questions carefully, read all the answer choices, and find the best answer (by eliminating the wrong answers, if necessary).

3. Have students take the sample test individually, filling in the appropriate circles to indicate their answer choices. This gives students practice in reading the questions and answer choices for themselves and marking an answer.

4. Group students based on their answer choices. That is, try to have students with different answers in each group. Have students explain to each other why they chose their answers.

5. Come back together as a class and discuss the types of questions on the test. Go through the test together, discussing how to determine the best answer for each question. Use this as an activity to have students learn about taking tests, not just finding the correct answers for this particular test.

   - *Question #1* is a compare/contrast question. Students can use what they already know about the region (background knowledge) to find the best answer. Students can use the keywords referring to landforms to skim the passage and discover that only one region has swamps.

   - *Question #2* asks students to recall a particular detail. The passage refers to crops growing in just one specific region, although crops grow in all areas of the United States. Students are asked to focus on a particular detail as it relates to the reading. Inform students that if a detail question refers to information mentioned in more than one paragraph of the passage, they can read the detail in context to determine the best answer for the question.

   - *Question #3* asks students to use context clues to answer the vocabulary question. They will have to read the other sentences in the paragraph to determine what the word means—an area of high, flat land. They can also substitute the answer choices in the sentence in the passage to determine which one makes the most sense.

   - *Question #4* asks students to identify the main idea of the reading passage. Have students refer back to the graphic organizer they completed as a class to determine the main idea of each paragraph. Students may also use context clues, such as the title of the selection, to identify the overall main idea.

   - *Question #5* asks students to make inferences. Remind students that they are looking for a sentence that is not true or less true than any of the others. Point out sentences in each paragraph that show how the climate differs from one region to another, indicating that answer choice A is not true. Have students look back over the passage to determine that rain falls in the West and falls very little in the Southwest, thus eliminating answer choice B. More than one paragraph includes mountains and different people groups, indicating that answer choices C and D are mostly true.

Closing

1. Have students talk with partners about one thing they learned about taking a test in this lesson. Have students share their ideas with the class.

2. Compile student responses to create a "Test-Taking Tips" class book to encourage students and give them confidence in test-taking situations throughout the year.

ELL Tips

✦ Break test directions into smaller "chunks."

✦ Give students another opportunity to practice test-taking skills using a different reading passage.

✦ Encourage students to use context clues (pg. 71) to answer vocabulary questions.

United States Regions

The Northeast has a rocky coastline along the Atlantic Ocean. There is farmland away from the coast. Four major rivers and two of the Great Lakes are in this region. The coast gets more rain than the farmlands. Most of the region gets snow, although the amounts vary. Summers are warm or hot and humid. Many people in the Northeast live in cities such as New York or Boston.

Many landforms exist in the Southeast. There are the Appalachian Mountains, Smoky Mountains, coastal areas, and swamps. The rest of the region is mostly plains. Winters are cool and mild with rain from storms out of the north. Summer weather is hot and humid. Thunderstorms and hurricanes bring rain and wind. African Americans, American Indians, and other people live here.

The Midwest consists of flat, grassy plains, lakes, and rolling hills, with more trees in the eastern part of the region. The Great Lakes are in the Midwest, as well as three major rivers: the Ohio, the Missouri, and the Mississippi. It rains more on the eastern side of the area than on the western side. It is cold and snowy in the winter and hot in the summer. Long ago, people from Europe settled in the Midwest. Many crops grow in this region.

There are mountains, coastlines, valleys, deserts, plains, and forests in the West. The different landforms affect the climate. Rain falls along the coast and in the valleys. Snow falls in the mountains. On the other side of the mountains, there are deserts. The Mississippi River forms the eastern boundary for the Western region. Other rivers flow through the West, including the Missouri, Colorado, and Columbia Rivers. Drought is common. Many groups of people live in the West, including American Indians, Latinos, and Asians.

The Southwest region has deserts, plateaus, and mountains. Plateaus are mountains with flat tops. There are dry, rocky hills and flat lands without much soil. Very little rain falls. The Rocky Mountain range runs through the northern part of the region. In some areas, it is cold in the winter. Many Latinos and American Indians live in the Southwest. Most people live in cities; not very many people live in the desert.

Name: _____ Date: _____

United States Regions

Directions: Read the selection. Use the passage to answer the questions. Fill in the circle next to the correct answer.

1. How is the Southeast region different from other regions?
   - Ⓐ It has mountains.
   - Ⓑ It has rain.
   - Ⓒ It has swamps.
   - Ⓓ It has different groups of people.

2. In which region do many crops grow?
   - Ⓐ Midwest
   - Ⓑ Southeast
   - Ⓒ Northeast
   - Ⓓ Southwest

3. In this passage, the word **plateau** means
   - Ⓐ a table with a plate on it.
   - Ⓑ an area of high, flat land.
   - Ⓒ a deep valley.
   - Ⓓ a place where people stand.

4. This passage is mainly about
   - Ⓐ where people live in the United States.
   - Ⓑ how many rivers are in the United States.
   - Ⓒ how much it snows in the United States.
   - Ⓓ the regions of the United States.

5. Which sentence is least true?
   - Ⓐ The climate of the United States is the same in every region.
   - Ⓑ It is drier in the Southwest region than in the West.
   - Ⓒ Many different people live in the United States.
   - Ⓓ The United States has many mountains.

United States Regions: Test Answers

1. C; It has swamps.

2. A; Midwest

3. B; an area of high, flat land

4. D; the regions of the United States

5. A; The climate of the United States is the same in every region.

Across the Curriculum *(cont.)*
Assessment

Assessing what students can and cannot do will help you to create focused learning experiences that are designed to take students to the next step in their learning. Once you have identified your students' needs, present curriculum accordingly. Plan assessments in such a way to allow students to express what they have learned. Assessments should reflect individual student growth, as well as the levels at which students have grasped particular concepts or skills.

When planning assessments, be aware of your students' . . .

✦ language proficiency levels.

✦ cultural backgrounds.

✦ educational backgrounds.

✦ learning styles.

✦ individual goals and needs.

✦ progress and growth over time.

Use a variety of procedures and techniques to assess students, such as the following:

✦ **Pre-Assessments**

- Oral diagnostics

- Simple written diagnostics

- Self-evaluation charts: Model for students how to use self-evaluation charts honestly while reading. Have students discuss later with a teacher.

✦ **Post-Assessments**

- Quick oral reviews

- Written work over time

- Observation charts or logs

- Exit tickets: Give students exit tickets. Have them respond orally or in writing to questions or prompts. Students give their tickets to the teacher on their way to another room or activity. Provide feedback as time allows.

- Student whiteboards: Discuss a problem or question. Have students respond on small student whiteboards.

- Comfort scale: Ask students to write or show a number of fingers to indicate the level of their understanding. (5 = I understand, 3 = I'm a little confused, 1 = I don't get it)

- Give One, Get One: Have students write or orally rehearse one new fact or piece of information they've learned. Go around the room asking students to add to a list compiled on the board.

- Think-pair-share (pg. 43)

Across the Curriculum *(cont.)*

Assessment *(cont.)*

Use a variety of procedures and techniques to assess students, such as the following:

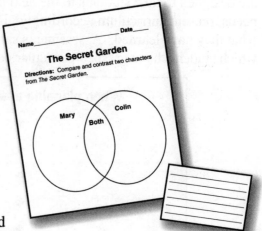

✦ **Pre- and Post-Assessments**

- Graphic organizers (pg. 32)

- Flash cards

- Quick writes or free-writing

- Journals

- Rough drafts

- Whole-group response (pg. 44)

- Class discussions

- Read-aloud comparisons: Have students read aloud and record their reading. Have students read the same passages at different times to compare fluency over time.

About Follow-up Assessments

Evaluate preliminary assessment results to determine what instruction is now needed to ensure that students meet stated standards or objectives. Write objectives for subsequent lessons that clearly state specific skills and content students should learn. Conduct follow-up assessments based on the following objectives:

- ✦ Help students identify their next learning steps.

- ✦ Give students appropriate tasks for their learning needs.

- ✦ Track student progress with ongoing assessments.

- ✦ Incorporate material already taught at students' levels to measure progress.

- ✦ Tell students your expectations prior to the lesson.

- ✦ Model tasks or activities first.

- ✦ Review assignments with students and check their answers.

Across the Curriculum *(cont.)*
Assessment *(cont.)*

Modify assessments as needed.

✦ Focus on student strengths rather than weaknesses.

✦ When possible, measure ELLs' progress individually, rather than measuring against native English speakers.

✦ Use assessments that don't always rely on student mastery of reading and writing.

✦ Modify test language and jargon.

✦ Simplify sentence structures.

✦ Adapt tests as needed to assess what students should be able to do.

About Standardized Testing

Educators recognize the need for accommodations in standardized testing procedures for students with limited English proficiency. Not all tests allow the same modifications. The questions below will help you determine how accurately a standardized test might measure ELLs' academic progress.

✦ Can teachers allow extra time for ELLs?

✦ Can students use bilingual dictionaries?

✦ Can students take the test in an alternate location that might be quieter or allow for oral testing?

✦ Can students take the test in a small-group environment?

✦ Can the test administrator read items orally to students?

✦ Can students respond to questions in their native languages?

✦ Can students use gestures, such as pointing or other physical demonstrations, to show learning?

Help students to reduce their test anxiety.

✦ Provide encouragement and support for students so they don't experience a fear of failure.

✦ Stress the importance of positive thinking.

✦ Talk to the parents of students who experience test anxiety. These students may feel nervous because they see their parents feeling this way. Alleviate everyone's fears by focusing on what the students know and what to expect on the test so they can study the unknown.

✦ Before testing students, teach them the following:

- the basics—where to write their names, how to follow directions (and read them carefully!), and how to fill in circles correctly
- academic language that will be on standardized tests
- types of test questions: true/false, multiple choice, fill in the blank, short answer
- ways to answer types of test questions
- the difference between facts and opinions
- how to skim and scan for information
- how to find the main idea
- how to find specific details
- how to make inferences
- how to find keywords and vocabulary
- how to sequence events
- how to compare and contrast
- to read all the answer choices
- how to eliminate wrong answer choices and find the best answer

---

About Grading

Grades are more than numbers or letters. Grading . . .

✦ is a communication tool that reflects your beliefs about learning.

✦ helps you to design appropriate tasks to meet student learning needs.

✦ gives students feedback and can request that students respond to feedback.

✦ should be based on clearly stated criteria for a task.

✦ gives teachers information for teacher/student conferences about specific student work.

✦ can incorporate checklists of increasing competencies.

✦ lets parents know their children's progress.

Across the Curriculum *(cont.)*

Assessment *(cont.)*

Encourage students to monitor their own learning.

✦ Have students complete the following sentence frames:

- Today I learned _____.

- When I didn't understand something, I _____.

- One thing I now know is _____.

- One new skill I learned is _____.

- I can use what I learned today to _____.

- I enjoyed discussing _____.

- One thing I will share with someone else is _____.

- Today's class was _____.

- I was feeling frustrated when _____.

- I would like to learn more about _____.

- One area in which I can improve is _____.

- If I was given the opportunity to do this again, I would _____.

- One of the difficult things about my project was _____.

Teacher Resources
Websites for Educators

Center for Applied Linguistics (CAL): *http://www.cal.org*
CAL publishes research, teacher education, instructional materials, etc., about language, literacy, assessment, and culture. For a complete list of their ELL resources, go to "TOPICS" at the top, left-hand side of the page and select "English Language Learners."

Classroom Zoom: *http://www.classroomzoom.com*
Classroom Zoom is an online subscription service created by Teacher Created Resources. Subscribers to the service have access to more than 11,000 printable lessons—all searchable by grade and subject. Members can also create custom crosswords, word searches, and math worksheets. Additionally, there are more than 1,000 free lessons available to nonmembers.

¡Colorín Colorado!: *http://www.colorincolorado.org*
This is a bilingual site created by WETA (Washington Educational Telecommunications Association) for families and educators of English language learners. It includes useful information, strategies, activities, and resources. Many activities have been designed for children in Pre-K–3 but can be adapted for older grades. Click on the "For Educators" link on the left-hand side to begin exploring many ELL resources.

Dave's ESL Café: *http://www.eslcafe.com*
This site is maintained by its founder, Dave Sperling—a teacher with both ESL and EFL instructional experience. Since 1995, Dave has devoted much time and energy to creating a site dedicated to providing ideas for ESL teachers, as well as support for ELLs. On this site, you can find teacher forums, lesson ideas, sample quizzes, and even job boards.

Everything ESL.net: *http://www.everythingesl.net*
Judie Haynes, an ESL teacher from New Jersey with more than 32 years of experience, is the main contributor to this site, which includes lesson plans, teaching tips, and various resources for ESL teachers. There is also a question-and-answer section where visitors are encouraged to ask questions (to Judie) and give responses.

LEARN NC: *http://www.learnnc.org*
LEARN NC is a program of the University of North Carolina at Chapel Hill School of Education. The site provides lesson plans, professional development opportunities, and innovative web resources to support teachers, build community, and improve K–12 education. To browse articles, tutorials, and books, click on "Best Practices" on the left-hand side.

National Center for Family Literacy (NCFL): *http://www.famlit.org*
NCFL has been promoting family literacy since 1989. It has helped more than one million families by pioneering family literacy programs. For free family and educator resources, including activities, tips, and podcasts, go to "NCFL IN ACTION" on the left-hand side, click on "FREE RESOURCES," and then select the topic of interest at the top of the page. Grant and professional development opportunities can also be found under "NCFL IN ACTION."

National Clearinghouse for English Language Acquisition and Language Instruction Educational Programs (NCELA): *http://www.ncela.gwu.edu*
This site contains information and resources dedicated to Title III (organized by state), standards and assessments, and grants and funding. It also offers webinars, publications (including NCLEA's *AccELLerate*), and a resource library to aid ESL teachers in the classroom. Use the search bar in the upper, right-hand corner of the main page to search by topic and access articles.

Reading Is Fundamental (RIF): *http://www.rif.org*
RIF is the United States's oldest and largest nonprofit children's literacy organization. Since its first distribution in 1966, RIF has continued to give new, free books to at-risk children. (In 2010, RIF gave more than 4 million children 16 million books!) For booklists, articles, and activities that inspire literacy, select "LITERACY RESOURCES" at the top of the page. RIF also provides training and resources to help parents and educators inspire children to read. RIF has 19,000 locations across the U.S. To find a RIF program near you, go to *http://map.rif.org/maps/* and type your ZIP code in the box.

Reading Rockets: *http://www.readingrockets.org*
Reading Rockets, a project created by WETA, is aimed to inform educators and parents on how to teach children to read, why some children struggle with reading, and how adults can help struggling children. The project includes PBS television programs; online resources, such as podcasts and blogs; and professional development opportunities. Strategies, reading guides, and newsletters can also be found on the site. For articles specific to ELLs, go to "Reading Topics A–Z" in the left-hand column and select "English Language Learners."

School Collection, The: Children's Literature at the Education & Social Science Library: *http://www.library.illinois.edu/edx/wordless.htm*
This site, which is maintained by the Education and Social Science Library at the University of Illinois at Urbana-Champaign, lists recommended wordless picture books appropriate for classroom use. The books are sorted by category, such as fantasy and adventure or animals.

Teachers First: *http://www.teachersfirst.com*
Helping educators since 1998, Teachers First offers teachers more than 12,000 classroom and professional resources, including rubrics, lesson plans, and tips for working with parents, substitutes, and technology.

Teaching Diverse Learners (TDL): *http://www.alliance.brown.edu/tdl/index.shtml*
TDL, supported by the Education Alliance at Brown University, is a website dedicated to providing support and resources for ESL teachers. It includes strategies, educational materials, and publications, as well as information on assessment and policy.

United Nations Cyberschoolbus: *http://www.cyberschoolbus.un.org*
This multilingual site offers accurate, official, and up-to-date information and statistics regarding the countries and cultures of the world. Visitors can learn about the history and work of the United Nations, as well as browse through UN publications, listen to webcasts, and read about the latest UN news.

Teacher Resources *(cont.)*
Translation Websites

Bing Translator: *http://www.microsofttranslator.com*

This free translator can translate over 30 languages. Users have the options of copying and pasting text into a box or entering website addresses (for full website translations). Additionally, the site offers Tbot—an automated "buddy" that provides translations for Windows Live Messenger. Using the Tbot translator, friends who speak other languages can have one-on-one conversations. Users simply need to add *mtbot@hotmail.com* to their Messenger contacts.

Dictionary.com Translator: *http://translate.reference.com*

This free translator can translate over 50 languages and up to 140 characters at a time. The site also offers a separate Spanish dictionary and translator. At the top of the page, select "Spanish" to view the translator box, as well as the Spanish word of the day, phrase of the day, and grammar tip of the day. The site contains over 750,000 English-Spanish dictionary definitions, example sentences, synonyms, and audio pronunciations.

Google Translate: *http://translate.google.com*

This free translator can translate over 60 languages. Users have the options of copying and pasting text into a box, uploading entire documents, or entering website addresses (for full website translations).

SDL FreeTranslation.com: *http://www.freetranslation.com*

This free translator can translate over 30 languages. Users have the options of copying and pasting text into a box or entering website addresses (for full website translations). The site also offers audio or emailed translations. A free iPhone application and Facebook translator can also be downloaded.

World Lingo: *http://www.worldlingo.com/en/products_services/worldlingo_translator.html*

This free translator can translate over 30 languages. Users have the options of copying and pasting text into a box, uploading documents, entering website addresses (for website translations), or entering email text (for email translations). Free translations are limited to 500 words.

Yahoo! Babel Fish: *http://babelfish.yahoo.com*

This free translator has a limited language selection; however, the site is very user-friendly. Users have the options of copying and pasting up to 150 words into a box or entering website addresses (for full website translations).

Teacher Resources *(cont.)*
Listening Websites

English Listening Quizzes: *http://esl.about.com/library/quiz/bllisteningquiz.htm*
This website includes more than 40 audio files along with matching quizzes. Quizzes cover a variety of topics, including ordering food, going on a trip, and finding out how much something costs. The language level is provided under each quiz and ranges from beginning to advanced.

Randall's ESL Cyber Listening Lab: *http://www.esl-lab.com*
Randall Davis, an educator with extensive ESL and EFL teaching experience, has been maintaining this website since 1998. The site includes more than 100 audio files (in both children's and adults' voices), as well as matching quizzes. The quizzes are categorized by topic (e.g., general, academic) and level (e.g., easy, medium, difficult) and can be graded electronically. Most quizzes are also accompanied by related pre-listening and post-listening exercises.

Tips for Online Searches

◆ Add "ELL" to any search term to narrow the focus.

◆ Search for any strategy, for example "ELL visualization" or "ELL environmental print."

◆ Look up the following keywords and phrases:

- literacy strategies
- learning styles
- cultural awareness
- culture and customs lessons
- signal words
- common idioms
- wordless picture books
- readers' theater scripts
- graphic organizers
- assessment

Note: Consider locating specific articles and then cutting and pasting the information into text or HTML documents (on a blog) for student use, as some advertisements may be inappropriate for younger students.

Bibliography

Adler, Mortimer J., Ph.D. "How to Mark a Book." The Radical Academy. Accessed July 25, 2011. http://www.tnellen.com/cybereng/adler.html.

Ben-Yosef, Elite. "Respecting Students' Cultural Literacies." *Educational Leadership* 61, no. 2 (October 2003): 80–82.

Fay, Kathleen and Suzanne Whaley. "The Gift of Attention." *Educational Leadership* 62, no. 4 (December 2004/January 2005): 76–79.

Haynes, Judie. "Teach to Students' Learning Styles." Everything ESL.net. Accessed July 25, 2011. http://www.everythingesl.net/inservices/learningstyle.php.

Lessow-Hurley, Judith. "What Educators Need to Know About Language." In *Meeting the Needs of Second Language Learners: An Educator's Guide.* Alexandria, VA: Association for Supervision and Curriculum, 2003.

Nieto, Sonia M. "Profoundly Multicultural Questions." *Educational Leadership* 60, no. 4 (December 2002/January 2003): 6–10.

Opitz, Michael F., and Lindsey M. Guccione. *Comprehension and English Language Learners.* Portsmouth, NH: Heinemann, 2009.

Project G.L.A.D. Accessed July 25, 2011. http://www.projectglad.com/

Quindlen, Terrey Hatcher. "Reaching Minority Students: Strategies for Closing the Achievement Gap." *Education Update* 44, no. 5 (August 2002).

Ren Dong, Yu. "Getting at the Content." *Educational Leadership* 62, no. 4 (December 2004/January 2005): 14–19.

Reyes, Carmen Y. "When Students Don't Get It: Helping Low Achieving Students Understand Concepts." Teacher Planet. December 29, 2009. Accessed July 25, 2011. http://www.news4teachers.com/When_Students_%20Dont_Get_It.php.

Sapon-Shevin, Mara. "Schools Fit for All." *Educational Leadership* 58, no. 4 (December 2000/January 2001): 34–39.

Simkins, Michael, Karen Cole, Fern Tavalin, and Barbara Means. "Making a Real World Connection." Chapter 3 in *Increasing Student Learning through Multimedia Projects.* Alexandria, VA: Association for Supervision and Curriculum Development, 2002.

Stephens, Peter. "How to Mark a Book." *Slow Reads Blog.* http://slowreads.com/ResourcesHowToMarkABook-Outline.htm.

TESOL. *TESOL ESL Standards for Pre-K–12 Students.* Alexandria, VA: TESOL, 1997.

Tomlinson, Carol Ann. "Grading for Success." *Educational Leadership* 58, no. 6 (March 2001): 12–15.

WIDA. "WIDA Performance Definitions." WIDA Consortium. Accessed July 25, 2011. http://www.wida.us/standards/PerfDefs.pdf.